TO: Jimmy

From: Melanie

X-mas 1981

A Boy's Albuquerque

The author at age eight.

A Boy's Albuquerque, 1898-1912

Kenneth C. Balcomb

Published in cooperation with the
Albuquerque Historical Society
by the

UNIVERSITY OF NEW MEXICO PRESS

Albuquerque

Library of Congress Cataloging in Publication Data

Balcomb, Kenneth C   1891–1979
   A boy's Albuquerque, 1898–1912.

   Includes index.
   1. Balcomb, Kenneth C., 1891–1979   2. Albuquerque,
N.M.—Biography.   3. Albuquerque, N.M.—History.
I. Title.
F804.A3B34   978.9′61 [B]   79-2774
ISBN 0-8263-0525-3

Photo Credits

The following institutions and individuals were generous in assisting the Albuquerque
Historical Society's photographic search and granted permission for the reproduction of the
following photographs:

Albuquerque Museum Photo Archives—1, 4, 5, 6, 15, 16, 17, 19, 21, 22, 23, 27, 28, 31
Zimmerman Library; Albuquerque Museum Photo Archives—3, 7, 12, 14, 26, 32
Zimmerman Library Special Collections—2, 8, 13, 18, 20, 24, 25, 29, 30, 33
Kenneth C. Balcomb—frontispiece, 9
Robert W. Cooper—10, 11

© 1980 by the University of New Mexico Press. All rights reserved.
Manufactured in the United States of America.
Library of Congress Catalog Card Number 79-2774
International Standard Book Number 0-8263-0525-3
First Edition.

Dedicated to my sister,
Marion,
who suffered through
my childhood experiences

Foreword

The Albuquerque Historical Society is pleased to join the University of New Mexico Press in the publication of these delightful recollections of Albuquerque as it was around the turn of the century. Seen through the eyes of a young boy growing up as our town was growing up, places and events take on a new perspective. Newcomer and old-timer alike should have a fresh appreciation of the changes that have occurred over the past one hundred years. To the words and incomparable sketches done by Mr. Balcomb, the Historical Society has added a selection of photographs of early Albuquerque. In this joint endeavor to make Kenneth C. Balcomb's memories available in printed form, the Society feels that it is fulfilling one of its prime objectives, that of preserving for this and future generations the history of Albuquerque. Surely this is a fitting contribution to the celebration of one hundred years since the coming of the railroad changed forever the town of Albuquerque.

Margaret H. Dike, President
The Albuquerque Historical Society

Introduction

Many delightful books and articles have been written about early Albuquerque, re-creating for us a view of life in this pioneer town—incidents, descriptions, and anecdotes, all illustrative of its people and early growth. To my knowledge, however, the story of early Albuquerque has not been told from a boy's point of view.

Things seem so large when one is young, but dwindle discouragingly when one gets older. Incidents, magnified in importance to a child, may lose this importance for adult. That which seems convulsively funny seldom retains its humor from an adult viewpoint. Nevertheless, it seems to me that an insight into these youthful reactions might hold important implications to anyone interested in a town's characteristics and growth, besides being amusing and appealing to readers. I am, therefore, impelled to write about them, even though now very much an adult.

This story of Albuquerque recalls some of the things I saw or heard of, some of my youthful reactions, and some of the people in Albuquerque between the years 1898 and 1912, by which time both the town and I had outgrown our youth. Though much personal history is included to give continuity and timing to the narrative, it is not intended as an autobiography, but rather as a biographical sketch of a town as it grew from a village to a small city. More than forty of my pen-and-ink drawings are included to give a visual impression of early Albuquerque.

It has been fun recalling these youthful experiences, and I am pleased to share them with readers. I recollect the men and women mentioned with fondness and respect; I sincerely hope readers will also gain an appreciation of them. There has been an added reward which I should, perhaps, mention. I am all the more convinced that there is a God in Heaven who looks after us; how else could a boy overcome all the hazards that beset him and grow to adulthood?

Kenneth C. Balcomb
September 1979

1

THE TRAIN ON WHICH MY SISTER AND I ARRIVED from San Diego slipped into the station in the dusk of a December evening in 1898. It was snowing, my first sight of snow. As we alighted on the board platform alongside the red frame depot, we were greeted by my father (whom I was seeing for the first time within my memory), a large and jovial man with a comfortably prominent middle section. He struck me as resembling Santa Claus, a prophetic illusion under the circumstances. It was cold, and our San Diego clothing seemed inadequate as we hurried across Railroad Avenue (present-day Central Avenue) and up North First Street to the shelter of the Thirion Hotel.

All this comes through to me in a haze of recollection. The cloudy sky, the snow, the muddy roadway of Railroad Avenue, the boardwalk leading up North First Street, and the massive, two-story building housing the Thirion Hotel. The hotel rooms were on the second floor. In the pale glow of carbon light bulbs hanging from the ceiling, the flight of steps seemed to rise up and up and up. I remember my father, preceded by the tall proprietor, Mr.

Thirion, struggling up the stairway with two suitcases, followed by my sister carrying bundles.

Some of my recollections of events leading to our coming to Albuquerque are vivid, but some details are fuzzy; dates fade into obscurity, when and where become uncertain. I had been told that I was born in Denver, Colorado, on June 13, 1891; and that when I was two-and-a-half years old my mother, because of ill health, took me together with my sister, Marion, who was nine years older than I, to San Diego to live with her mother.

I can remember when my mother died—I was five years old—and something of my life with my grandmother, until, in 1898, my father moved from Denver to Albuquerque and sent for my sister and me.

My first recollection of living in Albuquerque is our having moved into a three-room frame house on Keleher Avenue. It must have been just before Christmas in 1898, as my first memory of it was on Christmas Eve and Christmas Day. I had expressed a desire for Santa Claus (personified in my father) to bring me a red wagon and, to my unbounded joy, it was there on Christmas morning. It stands out as one of my most wonderful Christmas presents.

Our house was the first of two small frame houses north of a spacious home on the corner of Keleher and Tijeras avenues. The street was no doubt named for the big family of Kelehers who lived in the large house. I soon became acquainted with Jesse Keleher, a year or two older than I. In later years I was to learn more about the Kelehers—of their being pioneers in Albuquerque and prominent in its development. It was unfortunate for me that Will

Keleher, a cousin of Jesse's, did not also live in the big house instead of way off in the southern part of town. As it was, I did not profit by an acquaintanceship with this wise and stimulating character until much later in life.

A family named Westerfeld lived in the house to the north of us. They had a boy named Arthur, who was also about my age. Mr. Henry Westerfeld ran a cigar-manufacturing and tobacco store downtown, complete with a wooden Indian out front.

Keleher Avenue was a sandy trail winding north from Tijeras Avenue between the board fence of the two houses and a barbed-wire fence to the left. Across the fence was a weed- and brush-covered field extending to the west as far as a child's eye could see. Cattle ran loose in the field and were rounded up and branded when necessary—a miniature affair, no doubt, but a Wild West adventure to a child. Once a fire started in the field, causing the cattle to stampede through the barbed-wire fence and into the streets. It caused great commotion—a frightening and exciting experience.

The open field furnished intriguing spaces to explore with my wagon. I went farther and farther, always keeping an eye on the cattle, being sure that the distance from me to them was greater than from me to the fence. It was on one such foray that I met Tony Rossi. Tony, though diminutive, was an aggressive and pugilistic individual who delighted in establishing his fistic superiority over any newcomer to the neighborhood. As I was of an uncombative disposition, it didn't take him long to subdue me to my proper place among his associates. Although I later became good friends with Tony, I never quite got over this early impression of him.

In 1898–99, only the homes of the more affluent boasted running water, flush toilets, electric lights, and telephones. Certainly the two small homes on Keleher Avenue did not.

In our house, kerosene lamps served for lighting, a pitcher pump rising from the kitchen drain board served as the source of water, and a dishpan served as a sink. Disposal of dishwater was very elementary—one simply threw it out the door. The privy stood grandly on the back of the lot—a two-holer complete with crescent in the door.

These crudities in living conditions probably had more of an impact on my sister than they did on me, as we had been used to more modern conveniences in my grandmother's home in San Diego. It was all a lark to me, and Mrs. Westerfeld next door seemed reconciled to the meager facilities. I marveled at the

dexterity and force with which she could heave a panful of water into the backyard, while holding the door with one foot to keep it from slamming.

Mr. Westerfeld was accustomed to bringing home the day's receipts from the cigar store at night. Evidently, hoodlums became aware of this and occasionally tried to rob their house, particularly when Mrs. Westerfeld was there alone. She always seemed equal to the occasion, however. She was reputed among us boys to be a crack shot with a rifle and once demonstrated this when she interrupted a would-be burglar. He escaped by climbing over the back fence, but not before a shot from her rifle had severed a piece of his britches, pinning it to the fence. We viewed this evidence of her marksmanship with amazement and admiration, as did the policeman who came to investigate. At another time, Mrs. Westerfeld, with a pan full of dishwater, opened the door just as an intruder essayed to get in. Without hesitation, she let him have the water full in the face, causing him to beat a hasty retreat, coughing and spitting.

Despite these attributes, which so appealed to us children, Mrs. Westerfeld was a kindly soul and a wonderful help to her neighbors. Jesse Keleher befriended me; I also formed a friendship with Arthur Westerfeld that endured for half a century. Arthur later served as Albuquerque's fire chief for many years.

I first learned about the town when going around with my father, who was a contractor and builder, but I was later permitted to go

alone. The impressions I gained of the town and some of the people
are indelibly stamped on my mind.

Records show that in 1898 the population was about five
thousand. The principal improved street was Railroad Avenue,
extending from High Street on the east to Old Town on the west.
No streets were paved, but sprinkler wagons plied back and forth
daily to keep down the dust. When it rained, all streets became
muddy. I can remember enormous wagons loaded with huge sacks
of wool, pulled by two, four, or sometimes six oxen struggling and
slipping through the mud of Railroad Avenue—marvelous sights to
a boy. Most sidewalks, where there were any, were boardwalks.
Trash collected under them attracted rats, and trying to kill them
furnished great sport for boys. The station platform, some sidewalks, and most store entrances had stone slabs that were brought
to Albuquerque on flatcars of the Santa Fe Railroad, which had
opened up a sandstone quarry in the vicinity of a division point in
Arizona called Flagstaff.

The railroad depot was a red frame building. Big potbellied
stoves heated the large waiting room, ticket office, and baggage
room. The Harvey Eating House was in a similar building south of
the depot.

Most of the town's activities centered around the depot, from which business houses extended east and west. The bon ton residential areas were north on Second Street, on West Copper across from Robinson Park, south on Third Street and south on Arno, Edith, and Walter streets. The business section of town petered out between Third and Fourth streets on Railroad Avenue, but the boardwalk extended to Fourth and thence south to Gold Avenue.

The mystery of North Third Street did not at first enter the consciousness of a seven- and eight-year-old, but sly remarks of boys with whom I became acquainted soon charged me with curiosity about, and some awe of, this Red Light district. It was forbidden territory for decent folks, and especially children. This glamorous area extended on Third Street north of Copper Avenue for several blocks and east and west of Third Street on Copper and Tijeras avenues for short distances. It was a world apart—not so much evil as it was mysterious.

Other forbidden places for children were the many saloons along Railroad Avenue. On the south side of the street, the Sturges bar was at the corner of First, the Graham Brothers' saloon was at mid-block on the alley, Joe Barnett's St. Elmo was next to the Second Street corner, and George K. Neher's resplendent White Elephant was on the corner. Others were on the north side of the street. Although they appeared dead and discouraged by day, they were livened by electric lights by night. Many a male passed through swinging doors and into the lighted rooms amidst the sounds of music and clinking glasses. Youthful ears heard that each had a "ladies' entrance" at the rear and we wondered about that. I can remember that on Wednesday nights the St. Elmo displayed a huge on-and-off electric sign announcing "Keno Tonight." A saloon gambling attraction then, keno was the same as the innocent game of bingo, played at church affairs today.

Of great interest to us were the horse-drawn street cars that ran on narrow-gauge tracks from First Street to Traction Park in Old Town. They seemed to be huge affairs, pulled by enormous fat-rumped horses driven by giant men (I was shocked in later years when I saw one of the cars—long since out of service—and realized it was only about twelve feet long).

The arrival of a horsecar at First Street was an exciting experience for us. As it came rolling up Railroad Avenue, the driver would tramp on a pedal to clang a huge bell and draw the horse to a halt with a great flourish. When the passengers had

alighted, the driver would unhitch the horse and lead him to the other end of the car to be again hitched and made ready for another trip. After a short wait, the great bell would again be clanged, the reins flicked, and the horse would step out at his set pace down the well-worn path between the tracks.

Each passenger who alighted from the car had a certain aura, and as passengers boarded, we wondered where they were going and envied them their experiences.

After the car had started again, the driver would wind the reins around the brake crank, allowing the horse to proceed unattended while he walked back to collect a nickel from each passenger. The horse seemed to know as much about the routine as did the driver. He would proceed at his normal pace, and if he came to a cross street where a prospective passenger was waiting, he would stop at the appropriate place, then start again when the passenger had boarded.

The horsecars carried out their most spectacular operations when many New Towners wished transportation to attend some show at Traction Park. At such peak-load times, several cars would be put in service with two horses, one ahead of the other. People filled the cars, stood on the steps, sat in the windows, and even rode on top. The cars resembled huge porcupines and were a hilarious sight with people sticking out all over.

Later, when we lived on Fourteenth Street, one of our great amusements was to bait the horsecar driver. Such baiting in downtown areas would have resulted in our arrest, but Fourteenth Street was safely out of the reaches of the law. As a car passed, we would jump on the rear and bounce up and down and yell. When the driver came after us, we would jump off and holler "Whoa-whoa," causing the horse to stop. When the driver went front again to start the horse, we would repeat the performance. Of course all this made the driver profanely angry. One driver was a Mr. Ruiz. Years later Mr. Ruiz collected the garbage in our neighborhood, and one day I reminded him of our youthful merriment at his expense. He became apoplectic with anger, and I thought he would strike me. Thus do animosities as well as friendships endure.

The horsecars were for so many years an inseparable part of Albuquerque. I have long wondered why one couldn't be built for observation, or even for riding on—like the cable cars in San Francisco. I was pleased to learn recently that the Museum of Albuquerque has restored one of the old horsecars and that my vision of commemorating their era by bringing one back into service for historically-minded passengers may be partially realized.

My father seemed to know many people, and while going with him I met many of them. One was a Mr. Richards, employed by the Highland Hotel at John Street and Railroad Avenue. Although quite ill with consumption, or tuberculosis as it is now known, he loved to go hunting, but was too weak to carry his gun. Much to my delight, he enlisted my services to go with him and carry it. When an opportunity came to shoot, I would hand him the gun and he would proceed to the kill with unerring accuracy. Another character was Mr. James McCorriston, the cement contractor. His name can still be seen imprinted on sidewalks in town, a testimony to the quality of his work. Mr. McCorriston was enormously fat and when the Elks Lodge built a theater, they provided an especially large seat in the fourth row front to accommodate his bulk. It was said he paid an annual fee for it whether he attended shows or not. Mr. Frank Ralph, the plasterer, drove the most outstanding team of grays in town. At a time when a man's station in life was often judged by the horseflesh he drove, this distinguished him.

Perhaps the most interesting character among my father's friends was a Mr. Metcalf, who ran a typewriter exchange in the Gekler

Building at the corner of Gold Avenue and Fourth Street. He was a socialist (when such were an oddity in the land) and was the perennial candidate for territorial delegate to Congress on the Socialist ticket. He was also an avid whist player, and on many occasions my father and others would spend time playing with him in the back room of the store. I spent many hours waiting there for my father, and my recollection is that during the game Mr. Metcalf would hold forth on socialism. Looking back, I wonder if he made these opportunities to indoctrinate his associates.

The intricacies of whist and socialism were mostly over my head, and boring, but I heard Mr. Metcalf's preachments so many times that some of them sank in. It seems to me that most of the principles of social justice that he advanced have since been adopted. Thus it is that a man may live ahead of his time because of the ideas he believes in, but never live to see how greatly what he believed influenced the future.

The magnificent three-story red stone building cater-cornered from the Gekler Building was the home of the Commercial Club,

the forerunner of the Chamber of Commerce. Borders Undertaking Parlor was on the ground floor. One ascended to the Club rooms on the second floor by climbing a seemingly never-ending stairway. I often went there with my father. The climb caused my portly father to puff and blow, and upon reaching the room he settled into a heavy, leather-upholstered chair to have a drink and talk with fellow members. The talking seemed interminable and boring, but I enjoyed being there in the aroma of their tobacco smoke. There were sleeping rooms on the third floor, equipped with the customary white porcelain washbowl, pitcher of water, and chamber pot under the bed.

We lived on Keleher Avenue for only a few months before we moved into a frame house located on two acres of land just north of Railroad Avenue on Fourteenth Street. It was out on the other side of the cattle pasture. It was spring, 1899, and the trees in the orchard surrounding the house were in bloom. The B. W. Rhea family, who had three boys about my age, lived in a house on Railroad Avenue across the street from the Huning Castle. The Harwood Home for Girls, which we understood was run by the Methodist Church for homeless girls or as a boarding school for girls, was to the north.

When living on Keleher Avenue, I attended the Fourth Ward School on North Sixth Street and continued to do so after moving. Mr. C. Roy Kiger was principal of the school. Although he was a tough disciplinarian, I remember him favorably. His main form of punishment was to grab a student by the collar and shake him violently. It was a one-sided affair with a little fellow like Milton Ellsworth, but a bit more competitive when he tried it on a big boy like Arthur Bachechi. A Mr. Hawley ran a little sundry store south of the school, which he called Hawley-on-the-Corner. For a penny, one could get wonderful sweets—all-day suckers, licorice sticks, and jawbreakers. A most marvelous place run by a man who had no difficulty communicating with children.

At this school, I came to know Roman Hubbell of later Navajo trading post fame; Charley Mann and Arno Blueher, sons of produce farmers; Gladys Mandell, whose father ran a clothing store; Arthur McCollum, whose father later became a prominent educator in New Mexico. Others were Emil Coullodon, who became a prominent taxidermist; Tony Rossi, a tinner; Ed Doran, a Rhodes scholar and teacher; and Arthur Bachechi, a merchant. It was there that I had my first love affair, although the object of my affections, a pretty girl whose father was Mr. R. W. Hopkins, the postmaster, never knew it. Harking back to this youthful infatuation reminds me of the story of the boy who told his mother of his interest in a little girl in the neighborhood. His mother told him she was right then at the corner drug store and if he would run down there he could see her. The boy hurried away, but soon returned. When his mother asked him if he had seen the girl, he replied, "Yes, and if I hadn't hidden behind a post, she would have seen me too."

The Fourth Ward School figured prominently in my life until, in the sixth grade, we were transferred to the Central School at Third Street and Lead Avenue, which then housed the sixth, seventh, and eighth grades, and the entire Albuquerque High School.

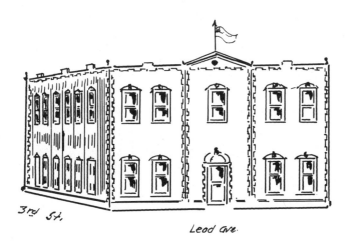

3rd St.

Lead Ave.

Living on Fourteenth Street furnished an eight-year-old boy interesting and amusing situations. The orchard provided a place to roam and play. It was only a block to Railroad Avenue and the horsecar tracks, and most important, it was only a block to the Huning Castle.

Just the name, Huning Castle, had a mesmeric effect on me. A castle! And although the castle's size dwindled as I grew older, it seemed enormous to an eight-year-old. Truly a castle! And in 1898–99 it was a busy place. Mr. Franz Huning was in evidence daily, a never-ending subject of awe. The orchard surrounding the castle was in active production. The lattice-covered walkway from the castle to a lake in the rear was still intact, grown over with

grapevines. The lake boasted water lilies and a canoe. It was truly a storybook place that we peeked at through an iron-grilled fence.

The Rio Grande was even then silting up its channel so that each spring's floods came nearer and nearer New Town. This encroachment was destroying Mr. Huning's back acres, which at one time had been great fields of hay and corn. A hog ranch was now operating farther back, from which the prevailing southwest winds brought a stench to complaining nostrils.

All this was new and exciting to me. Having been reared in the strict confines of my grandmother's home in San Diego, I now found adventure everywhere. The swampy lands furnished wonderful duck ponds where I went hunting with Mr. Richards. (It is hard to believe now, but the best pond of all was where Washington Middle School now stands.) And of course where there are fruit trees, as there were in the castle grounds, there is the temptation to the young to sample the crop. Just why we were prompted to steal Mr. Huning's fruit when we had fruit in our own orchard, I cannot now understand.

Tijeras Avenue gave some resemblance to a city street about as far as Eighth Street, but deteriorated into a sandy, winding road from there west. An abandoned two-story house, which we children called the "haunted house," stood on this sandy stretch, and coming home from school we took pains to give it a wide berth. Later this house was handsomely remodeled into the Neill B. Field home; but years later when I visited in their home, I always sensed a queasy feeling reminiscent of boyhood fears.

It was while we lived on Fourteenth Street that the Highland Hotel burned. When a fire occurred, a shrill siren sounded. As there was little between us and the town to obstruct the view, we could see the smoke from any sizable fire and then would run to it. The Highland Hotel fire was a major conflagration—it seemed everyone was there. My heart sank when I realized it was the Highland Hotel, the home of my hunting companion, Mr. Richards. (I cannot remember seeing him again.) Nevertheless, it was a splendid fire. The hotel had a well-stocked bar, and when the fire reached it, flames of various colors shot into the air—green, red, yellow, and purple—accompanied by explosions. I have always been curious to know which liquors caused which colors.

A great fire that I cannot remember was the one that destroyed the San Felipe Hotel. I have a faint recollection of this hotel being a three-story brick building on the southwest corner of Fifth Street and Gold Avenue. The Elks Theater later stood there (it also burned), then the Elks Club, and now a new Federal building. In his *Memoirs*, Will Keleher relates that when a boy he activated the fire-alarm box which gave notice of this fire. How I would have envied him this experience. I always looked with awe at the red fire-alarm boxes on telephone poles all over town and wondered what would happen if I broke the glass and pulled the switch.

2

In my eighth year I became acquainted with the Ellis Ranch and family. I feel that the story of the Ellis Ranch, tucked away as it is in a canyon in the Sandia Mountains, not more than twenty miles distant, properly belongs in a story of Albuquerque. The Sandia Mountains are to Albuquerque what Pikes Peak is to Colorado Springs—inseparable one from the other—and to my mind the Ellis Ranch is the heart of the Sandia Mountains.

Here in 1887 a family settled in an isolated and inaccessible mountain valley and developed a homestead out of the raw materials at hand, overcoming terrific obstacles with a native ingenuity reminiscent of the pioneers of a hundred years before. Theirs is a remarkable story of courage, tenacity, and prodigious effort.

I became intimately familiar with this family and ranch when, as a boy of eight through thirteen, I was privileged to live with them during summer vacation months. It began when my father agreed with Mr. Ellis that I could go to the ranch to be a companion to his son Paul, who was just my age. Also, I had been ill and Mr. Ellis convinced my father that a sojourn at the ranch would build up my health, which it did. It was in July of 1899 that I was introduced into the life of this remarkable family.

From what I can remember hearing, it seems the Ellis family lived in Kansas, but in 1887 came farther west seeking a better climate on account of Mr. Ellis' health. How he discovered the beautiful valley in the Sandias, I do not know, but he homesteaded 160 acres in 40-acre lots in such a way that, from the southwest corner of one 40 to the northeast corner of the last, his land included over a mile of Las Huertas Creek. The creek is unique in that, during flood periods, a heavy saturation of lime flows into it from a tributary. Below this tributary branches and debris which have lodged in the stream are encrusted and the lime forms dams that impound pools of crystal-clear water. Mr. Ellis used to say there were 160 pools on 160 acres. The stream formed the nucleus of an astonishingly beautiful canyon, bordered by fir, pine, oak, quaking aspen, and other varieties of trees and shrubs.

Mr. Ellis moved his family—his mother, wife, four sons, and two daughters—into this wilderness to live in tents until they could build a house. The oldest son, Guy, soon left to work for the railroad. The oldest daughter, Maud, married and followed her husband elsewhere, but the rest of the family stayed on.

No road led into the Sandias at that time. To get to their homestead, the Ellises traveled by wagon over a trail road through the Tijeras Canyon to La Madera, a little Mexican town on the east slope of the mountain some five miles from the ranch. There they left the wagons and packed their things on horses over a primitive trail to the ranch site. Furniture, stove, anvil, forge, bedsprings, and a myriad of items were thus transported. This was the manner in which I was transported—by buckboard to La Madera and then behind Mr. Ellis on one of the big black mares for my first horseback ride over the mountains. I stayed about five months this first time, leaving just before Christmas when the snow was two feet deep.

Mr. Ellis and the older sons became master craftsmen with the ax, cross-cut saw, adz, and blacksmith and carpenter tools. They cut and hewed pine trees for logs with which to build an eight-room house, a barn, and a chicken house. In a saw pit, with one man on top and one below, logs were sawed into boards for flooring, cupboards, doors, and furniture. Sawed sections of logs were split to make shingles for roofing. Five-gallon kerosene cans were fashioned into bathtubs, buckets, washbasins, and all manner of household utensils. Soft limestone was sawed into slabs for paving the ground floors and into blocks for building fireplaces in most rooms. Many years before, a mining company had attempted to construct a flume to carry water from Las Huertas Creek to the placer mine at Golden. From the abandoned line, the Ellises salvaged lengths of the pipe for chimneys, culverts, and watering and feed troughs.

The whole of what became a lovely and livable home was thus fashioned by prodigious labor and great skill, a minimum outlay of money, and little importation of material.

Many acres of fields were cleared for growing wheat, oats, hay, potatoes, and a large variety of vegetables. The irrigation system devised to water the steep hillside fields was ingenious, allowing saturation of soil without erosion. Large wooden-wheeled carts were built, to be pulled by a team of steers, for transportation within the ranch.

By 1899, a sizable herd of cattle had accumulated, milk cows to produce milk, butter, and cottage cheese; and steers for work animals and beef. The products of the ranch were supplemented with game taken by the older boys, Augie and Frank. They were great hunters and there was an abundance of game in the mountains—including bear, deer, wild turkey, and grouse.

There was a post office and a small store in the picturesque Mexican village of Las Placitas, six miles by tortuous trail down Las Huertas Canyon. A weekly chore for Paul and me was to ride steers equipped with uncomfortable packsaddles to get mail and such produce as flour, sugar, salt, kerosene, and "shorts" (the screenings of ground wheat midway between bran and flour, which were cooked for cereal). These were packed on the steers for the long walk back.

Mrs. Ellis, perhaps then in her late forties and a wonderfully happy and motherly soul, was a marvelous cook and clever seamstress. With the aid of her equally clever daughter Charlotte (whom we called Charlie), she provided sumptuous meals and clothed the family. As Paul had no chance to attend regular school, Charlie taught him school subjects in pace with the curriculum of public schools. It was much easier for her to keep his interest when I, or some other visiting boy, was there, so we had school every weekday morning—grammar, reading, writing, spelling, and geography; and such was her artistry as a teacher that we enjoyed it. Paul was later able to enter the eighth grade in Albuquerque schools.

A most vivid remembrance of this first stay was our Saturday night baths. The kerosene-can bathtub (made by soldering two kerosene cans together with a wooden rim around the top) just fitted the contours of an eight-year-old. Grandma Ellis bathed us in water heated on the kitchen stove. We would draw straws to see which would bathe first, both using the same water. There was much hilarity, followed by scolding from Grandma.

My Ellis Ranch experience was a rare privilege. It not only contributed to my health, but gave me lifelong pleasures and appreciations. We learned about trees and flowers and grasses. We learned the call of the coyote, the cry of the mountain lion, where turkeys roosted, and which springs bears and cats frequented. Charlotte Ellis was a competent amateur botanist, having discovered and classified several flowers—and she taught us. Present-day vacationers, speeding over mountain roads, galloping horseback over finished trails, or riding on chair lifts for miles in order to ski rapidly down slopes, miss something. They miss both the pleasure and knowledge to be had from carefully observing nature while hiking over mountains. The present-day trend of back packing, though, gives promise of greater dividends from nature.

The passing of time brought changes to the family and ranch. Grandma Ellis was buried in a plot on the place and several years later Mr. Ellis was buried alongside his mother. After his death, the family scattered and the ranch was sold to the late Reverend Hugh Cooper to become a Presbyterian conference grounds. The only remaining member of the original family is Paul, who returned to live on the place for a time.

3

WE MOVED AGAIN—this time to a brick house on the corner of Thirteenth Street and Roma Avenue (1300 West Roma). The move was probably made to obtain larger quarters when my two brothers, Spencer, five years my senior, and John, thirteen years older than I, came to live with us. This was our first house with indoor plumbing. At the rear of the lot was a two-story barn, the underneath for horses, and the upstairs for hay. The palatial home of Mariano Otero was on the lot to the south, and his much more pretentious two-story barn was nearly against ours. Mr. Otero, a roly-poly, very important-looking man was heir to the Baca Location Number One Grant in the Jemez Mountains. He must have had access to many piñon trees as the attic of his barn was full of huge sacks of these delicious nuts, so new to us. Spencer and I discovered this, and that a window in the second story of the big barn was opposite and about level with one in ours. We managed to span the gap between to pilfer all the piñons we could eat.

We were greatly impressed by Mr. Otero and the men, women, and young folks who frequented his home. Mr. Otero seemed always to be dressed in a black coat, pinstriped trousers, and plug hat. He wore high-heeled shoes, we assumed, to make him appear taller. His carriages were splendid and drawn by magnificent horses. He seemed always to have a driver and a footman just like those the storybooks told about. When he and his lady would emerge from the great front door to go riding, the footman would place a stool to assist their stepping into the carriage. It was impressive. An attorney named John Baron Burg had married one of the Otero daughters and he, likewise in splendid clothes, was much in evidence about the place.

Then there were the Harrison boys. They were sons of Dr. G. W. Harrison, who had married an Otero daughter. Those boys were the crowning envy of us who lived next door. They had a mini-buggy, called a gig, in which two small people could ride alongside each other, but with one facing forward and the other backward. The seat was upholstered in yellow straw, the rig was trimmed in red, and the Shetland pony that pulled it was brown with white dapples and a flowing white mane. I determined that someday I would have such a rig, but by the time my fortunes might have permitted it, horses and buggies, no matter how splendid, had given way to automobiles.

Pearce Rodey was often a visitor at the Oteros'. He was quite large for his age. In short pants, which all boys wore at his age, and with his massive shoulders, he was quite impressive. This impression was enhanced when I learned that his father, Bernard S. Rodey, a prominent attorney, was New Mexico's delegate to Congress for four years. He was the principal influence in having the territorial legislature provide for a university at Albuquerque, for which he was memorialized by Rodey Hall at the University of

New Mexico. I was to become a close personal friend of Pearce Rodey after he graduated from Harvard Law School and became a prominent Albuquerque attorney.

Two girls who quite often appeared at the Otero home (and whom I idolized from afar) were the Childers twins, Agnes and Edith. I think they lived in a two-story rock house where Mr. M. L. Fox later lived. I never quite overcame my awe of these pretty twins, even after I came to know them in later years.

While we lived on West Roma, my sister attended the University, riding a horse sidesaddle up the sandy, winding road.

There was no mail delivery in those days, so everyone had to go to the post office for mail. The post office was in the ground floor of a two-story brick building at the corner of Second Street and Silver Avenue. Doctors' and lawyers' offices were upstairs. Farr's Meat Market was three doors north and the First National Bank was on the corner of Second Street and Gold Avenue. M. P. Stamm ran a wholesale fruit and vegetable store across the street from the post office. We boys would watch the Stamm boys, Roy and Raymond, throw apples from a wagon into barrels, because they would often throw an apple to each of us.

There were many grocery stores to provide abundant food for Albuquerqueans. Jaffa's Grocery was where the First National Bank was later built, and the San Jose Market was farther east in the same block, next to Mr. Westerfeld's cigar store. The Trotter brothers, Frank and Hugh, ran competing stores, one on Gold and one on Railroad Avenue. The Skinners, Mr. A. J. Maloy, Mr. William L. Hawkins, and the Palladinos were pioneers in the grocery business in Albuquerque. These stores were forerunners of first, the cash-and-carry stores, and later of the supermarkets of today. Their approach to selling was different, however. They either solicited your business by sending order takers to your home in the morning and delivering the order in the afternoon, or by solicitously waiting on a customer when he went in to shop. Charge accounts were the ordinary way of business and when a customer paid his bill, he was given a box of candy.

Men's clothing needs were furnished by Washburn's, at Second and Gold, by "Simon Stern, The Railroad Avenue Clothier," and by Mike Mandell, whose store was sandwiched between Graham Brothers' bar and the St. Elmo saloon.

I can remember J. H. O'Rielly's and B. Ruppe's drug stores and that they sold drugs, cosmetics, candy, and ice cream, but—unlike such stores today—they left the selling of hardware, furniture, and garden tools to others.

A store that was a combination department, sundry, and grocery emporium was The Maze, run by Mr. William Kieke. It was located in the 200 block on South First Street and endured for many years—as long as Mr. Kieke endured. One could shop in The Maze and come out with anything from a sack of marbles, to a hair ribbon, to a hambone. The store had an interesting, musty atmosphere about it and attracted customers from all parts of town.

Montgomery Ward & Company announced in their 1972 advertising that they were in their second hundred years of operation. Reading this aroused nostalgic feelings, because before the development of present-day shopping centers catering to every human need, Montgomery Ward and its catalog were as indispensable as sunshine. Our clothes, our farming tools, the poultry and the grain to feed them—all were obtained by ordering from the catalog. We then waited anxiously until the items arrived by railroad express (this was before parcel post). The catalog was a wondrous thing to a child. It served as our storybook to be shown and read to us; and on

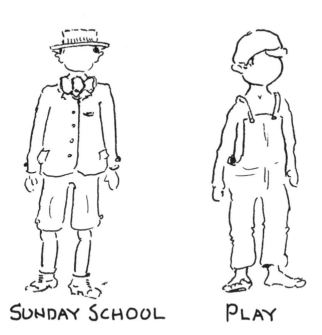

SUNDAY SCHOOL   PLAY

stormy days, we lay indoors on our stomachs perusing its pictures, transported to faraway places, and in our imaginations, equipped in splendid raiment. And, as a final token of usefulness, no privy was complete without a catalog hung on the wall.

In those early days, a family depended upon the skill of its female members with the needle and thimble to make and maintain a large part of their clothing. This required a source of supply for materials—piece goods, braids, thread, and all the findings required by a seamstress. Mr. and Mrs. David H. Boatright's store on West Gold Avenue furnished the ladies a one-stop source of these supplies. The store was called The Racket. We could not understand the significance of the name, but joked that it was from the clamor that came from the feminine voices of its customers.

Women's fashion in that period was severe by comparison with today's styles. Ladies wore steel-stay corsets that had to be tightened by a helper putting his foot on the rump and pulling the strings by might and main, accompanied by much grunting and groaning. Husbands came in very handy for this. These corsets were instruments of torture (for the sake of style), in the same class as

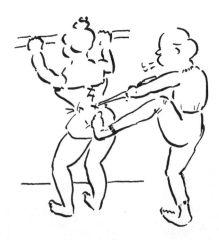

were binding shoes for Chinese girls. Women wore high-heeled, high-button shoes, hidden by sweepingly long dresses, which were padded by bustles for those slim in the rear. Their hats were huge affairs usually adorned with ostrich feathers, ribbons, or cloth flowers. They were held on by long hatpins sticking through the hair (usually padded by a "rat"). The pins were sometimes quite fancy and, it was rumored, could serve the double purpose of holding on the hat or acting as a weapon of protection.

A saloon called Zeiger's Cafe was in the two-story brick building later occupied by the Albuquerque National Bank. Doctors' and lawyers' offices were on the second floor, reached by steep steps at the rear. The Bank of Commerce was across the street to the west. It was run by Mr. W. S. Strickler, whose boy, Kennedy, went to school with me. A dry goods store called The Golden Rule was on the corner of Third Street and Railroad Avenue, and there were two others across the street, the most long-lived of which was The Economist.

On North Second Street where the Plaza Hotel now stands was Trimble's Livery Stable. Here one could board a horse or rent a saddle horse or a horse and buggy. Mr. W. L. Trimble ran stages, a fleet of drays, and rented a huge tallyho, which would hold twenty or thirty persons. We boys loved to walk past the big front door of the large-fronted frame building, peeking into the dim interior and breathing the comfortable odors that emanate from stables. Mr. Trimble, a portly man, usually well-dressed and wearing a derby hat, would stand out front and greet passers-by. A bright gold watch chain hung across his front, protecting a pocket watch in one vest pocket and some trinket in the other.

Across the street to the north of Trimble's was the Strong Brothers' Undertaking Parlor and Furniture Store. The Undertaking Parlor (the forerunner of the Strong-Thorne Mortuary) seemed to be the principal concern of Mr. Harry Strong, with Mr. Frank Strong handling the furniture business. They were real pioneers, having come to Albuquerque with their parents when quite young. Mr. Harry Strong delighted in telling us boys of Indian raids in the outlying parts of the town in the early days.

Across the street from Strongs' was a large depressed area where Mr. Trimble stored wagons and drays. When it rained, the vehicles would be standing in water. I think Mr. Korber had his first blacksmith shop at the edge of the sunken area. At any rate, I saw this one-man enterprise grow to a block-square complex, J. Korber & Company, which came to sell everything from hardware to paints and from furniture to automobiles. It started with the two-story Korber Building on the corner of Second Street and Tijeras Avenue, which housed a fabulous hardware store. Offices were upstairs. Later the city rented a part of the building for the city hall, jail, and fire department, until the splendid new City Hall building was built across the street. Korber's eventually added the rest of the block to their holdings, including the Kennedy-Strickler building at the corner of Second Street and Copper Avenue.

North of the depression, across Tijeras Avenue among cottonwood and willow trees, was the city jail. Painted an unpleasant green, it seemed a pitifully small affair even to a child's eyes. I can remember it having only one room, although I am sure this was not the case. It had ominous-looking bars at the windows and doors. We avoided the jail like a pesthouse, but took a lively interest in the activities of the policemen, whose headquarters were somewhere in the vicinity of the jail. The chief of police, Mr. Thomas McMillin, was handsome and athletic looking. He wore a shiny gold star on his immaculate blue uniform and was greatly admired as he strode gracefully around town. I particularly remember two policemen, Lewis A. Knapp, who had a very prominent bay window—we would wonder how he could run fast enough to catch a miscreant—and Tony Rossi's father, a friend to us kids, especially on Halloween night.

The police paddy wagon was a single horse-and-buggy rig that we called the "hurry-up" wagon. One would sometimes see a policeman driving towards the jail with one arrestee beside him on the seat and another one or two sitting in the back with their feet hanging out.

Our greatest interest was in the Fire Department. The fire engine and the horses that pulled it were the wonder of wonders, and the firemen were all heroic figures. Although I do not remember where they were housed, I vividly remember the huge black, fat-rumped horses being stalled alongside the fire engine with their harness suspended above them. When an alarm sounded, the harness dropped, firemen buckled the necessary straps, the bar in front of the horses would rise, and each horse, without prompting, stepped forward to his place in front of the vehicle. Neck yokes and tugs were fastened, the lines handed to the driver, and with a loud clanging of a bell on the vehicle, the horses charged into the street with firemen jumping onto their stations on each side. All this took about the time it took to count to twenty.

The fire engine was essentially a steam-generating plant and a pump that was run by the steam. It had a huge bottle-shaped boiler with a firebox underneath. The neck of the bottle was the chimney out of which smoke belched as the contraption went streaming down the street with bell clanging. In some way a fire was always kept burning under the boiler so that, when on a run, a fireman had only to shovel in coal (from a coalbox on the rear of the

vehicle) to generate steam by the time they reached the scene of the fire. The whole procedure was a wonderful example of precision training of men and horses. We would hang around the station hoping an alarm would ring so we could see them go.

Another alarm that had a profound effect in the lives of us boys was the "curfew bell." It hung in a steel derrick located in the vacant lot at the corner of Railroad Avenue and First Street where the Y.M.C.A. was later built. It was rung at 8:00 P.M. as a signal for young people under sixteen to be off the streets unless with an adult. It was also rung in emergencies such as flood or fire, or on such festive occasions as July Fourth, or when there was a parade. The bell, sitting high in its derrick, had a peremptory effect on us boys. It seemed to carry an authority almost human. As we passed it even in daytime we looked up at it with the respect due a judge or other officer of the law.

The whistle at the Santa Fe Railroad shops also held an important place in all our lives. The sound of this deep-throated signal to shop workmen could be heard for miles, and it essentially started and ended everyone's day. Shop employees worked a ten-hour day, 7 A.M. to 6 P.M. The whistle blew twice at 6:45 A.M. to tell them to get on the job, and once at 7 o'clock telling them to get to work. Railroad time was the most accurate time we could get, so everyone set his clock or pocket watch, and started his day's activities, by the shop whistle. When it blew repeatedly at other times, we knew something special was afoot: a fire, a flood, the arrival of a special dignitary. It talked to us. Its importance, in addition to its functions, was of course that it represented the Santa Fe Railroad, around which the life of the community revolved during its first fifty years.

Records show that the first passenger train arrived in Albuquerque on April 22, 1880. I am sure this event caused as much excitement in the small village as the arrival of a train did in 1898–99, when it was an occasion of interest and excitement for young and old. There were west-bound and east-bound trains, and all stopped at Albuquerque to change engines and crews, replenish supplies, clean up, and to give passengers a chance to eat.

Transportation by train was the only reasonably fast means of getting anywhere, whether to Bernalillo, Belen, El Paso, Los Angeles, or New York City. Each day people were going someplace, or arriving from a trip, and friends gathered to say goodbye, or to welcome someone home. Many days a train carried a notable, whose arrival, heralded by the papers, caused a crowd to gather. We small folks tried to be on hand on such occasions, when we weren't in school.

I well remember the passenger cars. Compared with today's comfortable, temperature-controlled silver monsters, they were crude affairs—dark green and of wood construction, with no ventilating or cooling systems, necessitating opening windows for fresh air (and soot and cinders). People alighting from the train sometimes looked as if they had been through a dust storm. But it was all wonderful to us.

My first recollection of a Harvey House was after the Alvarado Hotel was built in 1901–02. The organization which enabled the feeding of one or two hundred passengers was remarkable, and during a twenty-minute train stop resulted in pleasant dining. A large brass dinner gong would sound as the train pulled in; passengers would rush to the already set tables; food would be served piping hot and without any evident fuss or turmoil. The meal would proceed smoothly and be completed by the time the conductor's cheerful "Board!" sounded, and all would stroll back to their cars well fed and satisfied.

The tracks and depot were level with the surrounding country. There was no underpass, and gates went down on Railroad Avenue when a train approached. The visible activities of train arrivals are pictured nostalgically in my mind, but memories of the sounds come back vividly also: the whistle as the train approached in the distance, growing ever louder as it neared; the engine bell ringing; steam hissing from places all over it; and brakes slipping and squealing as the train stopped unerringly in front of the depot. Immediately, organized pandemonium broke loose. Baggage trucks were pulled about, with the men shouting at one another. The Harvey House gong sounded peremptorily, newsboys called their extras, and people shouted and squealed as they greeted each other. And always could be heard the deep, resonant voice of a hotel barker booming out "Savoy Hotel." When a returning passenger heard that call, day or night, he knew he was back in Albuquerque.

To adult citizens of the growing city, the replacement of the old red frame depot with the resplendent Alvarado Hotel was no doubt of momentous importance, but it was not until I was much older and could participate in events at the Alvarado that its full significance in the life of the town became apparent to me. The advent of this beautiful gray hotel, eating house, and depot comes to me in haze of recollections along with the change of the name of Railroad Avenue to Central Avenue, the replacement of horsecars with electric trolley cars, the paving of Central Avenue, the laying of cement sidewalks, and the displacement of horses and wagons by automobile traffic. We grew up with these changes, having no hand in their development; for us, they just occurred and became a part of our lives.

WHILE LIVING ON FOURTEENTH STREET, I found an old frame of a lady's bicycle and undertook to make a usable unit of it. By dint of scrounging and buying parts, I finally rebuilt it. I got more pleasure from that bicycle than from any of the grander ones I had later. It was during this effort that I became acquainted with Tom Insley, who ran a bicycle shop on West Gold Avenue. Several years later, Tom shot his brother-in-law with both barrels of a double-barreled shotgun, for which he was put in the penitentiary at Santa Fe. Notwithstanding this unfortunate ending, Tom was a wonderful friend to us boys. His shop was a hangout, and he took great interest in keeping our dilapidated bicycles running.

This was the day of bicycles. Men rode them to their offices and ladies went shopping on them. Kids rode to school on "bikes," and the ultimate was for a suitor to arrive for his lady with a tandem built for two, the back part equipped to accommodate her.

Bicycle races were a major sporting event, with minor competition throughout the year culminating in a race to the mountains in the spring. It was a grueling event through winding, sandy, and rutted roads, ten miles up and ten back. This was always a gala occasion. The participants trained for weeks in advance; many started the race, but only a few would finish. A young man by the name of Harvey Bittner usually won, and he was a hero whom all small boys worshipped and tried to emulate. We, too, would stage races, but they usually ended with broken bikes or flat tires.

Tom Insley got one of the first horseless carriages to come to Albuquerque. They were called horseless carriages because they looked like carriages without singletrees and shafts and, of course, the horse. Compared to today's beautiful cars, his was a funny-looking contraption, but it was a thing of wonder and beauty to us. The car was started by spinning a crank that projected from the side. The engine would pop and hiss and churn in a veritable uproar of excitement when it would finally consent to start. It smelled bad, scared horses, and was cussed more than admired.

A popular story at that time was of the preacher who observed a group of small boys playing in a peculiar formation, and stopped to inquire about the game. They explained that they were playing horseless carriage, each one representing a part of the car—crank, wheels, body, and so forth. The preacher smiled and walked on, but soon came to a boy all alone. "Why aren't you playing with the other boys?" he inquired, whereupon the boy explained that he *was* playing with them—he was the car's smell!

A memorable day for us was the time Mr. Insley tried to negotiate the twisting, sandy roadway of Tijeras Avenue in his horseless carriage. The vehicle had a contrary steering apparatus

and small, solid-rubber tires on huge spoked wheels—definitely not designed to run in sand. Just as he was in front of the "haunted house," the front wheels twisted and the engine gave a discouraged cough and stopped; the car was hopelessly stuck. Several of us had trailed along, as we could run as fast as the machine would go, so we were on hand at the denouement, much to Tom's relief. It took all his mechanical genius, plus the push of a half-dozen boys, to get the car rolling again. We were enormously proud to have been a part of this experience and bragged about it.

Natural gas for stoves and heating was unheard of in 1898–99, but we did have a gas system of limited distribution, mostly for lighting. Both gas and electricity were generated at the corner of Railroad Avenue and Broadway. We understood that gas was derived by heating soft coal without enough air to let it burn. In the process, there was a by-product of tar that ran out on the adjacent lot in a great gooey mess. We attempted to chew some, but found it a poor substitute for gum. Remnants of tar remained on the ground for years.

A continual bone of contention in the town was the inadequacy of the water system. Although I knew little about all this, I was aware that the system was owned by an attorney named A. B. McMillen. He received much public criticism because of the uncertainty of the water supply, but I had a feeling of hot loyalty for Mr. McMillen because he gave me a job helping to prepare his white greyhound bitch dog for shows. Mr. McMillen was a large man who lived in a big house on South Walter Street and had saddle horses and a pack of greyhounds. With his wife and daughter Aileen riding sidesaddle, he would ride on the mesa beyond the University to let the dogs chase rabbits. His being able to make such excursions was, in my young viewpoint, the ultimate mark of opulence.

The white female greyhound was evidently a particularly fine specimen and took ribbons at the shows. I cannot recall how I got a job helping to prepare the dog, but I do remember it was a quite meticulous task. She had first to be bathed with a special soap and thoroughly dried and examined. Then she was rubbed briskly with sandpaper to make her pink skin show through the white hairs. I loved dogs and enjoyed it all, except the sandpapering. It hurt me more than it seemed to hurt the dog. Mr. McMillen personally trained the dog in the proper stance and actions for the judging ring. He was very stern, but always kind, with the dog and with me.

The corner lot where the Rosenwald Building was later built was sunken considerably below the walk level forming a natural amphitheater, and it was used as such when noted speakers came to town. I remember hearing Theodore Roosevelt and William Jennings Bryan speak there. Mr. Trimble would place a large dray in the depression to serve as a speaker's platform, with steps at each end so that people could ascend and shake the speaker's hand. The audience stood on the slopes of the depression, or on the adjacent boardwalks. We boys climbed the steps to shake hands with both Mr. Roosevelt and Mr. Bryan.

Probably, if one should delve into the origin of any modern town, he would find that some enterprising soul, with profit in mind, had subdivided a piece of ground and induced people to buy lots. From this nucleus these additions spread outward as other promoters subdivided adjoining acres to sell more lots. Sometimes it was generally conceded that such entrepreneurs served a good and timely purpose, but in other cases, they were considered visionary and impractical. I heard this issue of land development discussed by my father and his friends. The consensus seemed to be that Mr. Huning, in developing the area east of the railroad to High Street (naming the streets after his children Arno, Edith, and Walter), had been timely with his project. They seemed to agree, however, that Mr. Stamm (of the wholesale fruit and vegetable store) was "way out" in trying to develop the area south of Railroad Avenue and east of High Street, to what later became Yale Avenue. This did seem way out, even to a child, considering that it took an hour with horse and buggy to struggle through the sandy streets he had scraped out to get to his headquarters. And with what seemed more courage than wisdom, he drilled a deep water well in a fenced square-block area where the Technical Vocational Institute now stands, erected a huge water tank, and planted many fruit and shade trees. He also extended complete, but inadequate, water mains down East Gold, Silver, Lead, and Coal avenues. In doing all this, Mr. Stamm may have been considerably ahead of the times, but in years later when we lived on lovely East Silver Avenue, we appreciated his foresight and courage.

The development of other attractive areas through the years attests to the courage and vision of other subdividers. Perhaps some had visions in advance of need, but without such enterprise, towns could not grow in an orderly fashion. Even though much of the population that settled in these new areas lived outside the restricted city limits, and did not show up in the city's population records, these additions contributed to the eventual betterment of the community.

The presence of the Red Light district on North Third Street was something I heard discussed pro and con. Those against the district abhorred its tolerance and carried on constant agitation for closing it. The women of the district were licensed to carry on by the city government, strictly regulated, and subjected to periodical medical examinations to reassure patrons that there was no presence of venereal disease. With this in mind, those who advocated continuing the district maintained that this type of activity on the part of females would continue whether or not they were districted and licensed, and it was better to assure healthful conditions by having them under close scrutiny.

All this came to me little by little, not fully understood, but tantalizingly interesting. We could see the "painted ladies" walking to town to shop. They were required to walk at least four paces apart. One could identify them by this separation and by their dress. Today, with styles as they are, these painted ladies would not be conspicuous; but in those days, their rouged cheeks, painted lips, darkened eyelashes, huge hats, bustles, and highly colored dresses made them stand out.

The Red Light district was an issue in every election campaign for mayor and aldermen, and finally enough sentiment against its continuance was aroused to elect a mayor pledged to close it. I think his name was Boatright. So the district was closed and "To Let" signs appeared in the windows of the former "cribs." We wondered what had become of the tenants.

This did not permanently settle the issue. During a later campaign in which a Red Light district was made a principal issue, the pros won, electing a mayor pledged to its reopening. The "To Let" signs came down and the controversy started all over again. Finally the district was again closed and has remained so, although the advisability of strict regulation of this "oldest of trades" is still debated.

5

My father was a contractor and builder, but it seemed his first love was mining. In his varied career, he had rushed to several strikes in California and Mexico, the Bisbee and Tombstone strikes in Arizona, the Cripple Creek and Leadville booms in Colorado, and any others he had heard of. He, and others, believed that the Sandia Mountains were mineralized, and he visualized the need of a smelter strategically located to process the ore that was sure to be developed. The site he decided on was at Algodones, twenty-three miles north of Albuquerque. He bought land there, built a house, and moved my sister, brother Spencer, and me up there in the fall of 1899. I was destined to live there for three years.

While living in Algodones, Spencer and I attended the small school where instruction by a Mr. Hovey was carried on in Spanish. Spelling was taught with the whole class singing the letters in unison. In learning, for example, to spell the Spanish word for monkey, *mono*, we would sing out: *"emmy o, mo; enney o, no; mono."* It was entertaining as well as instructive. The school was next door to the Catholic Church, and whenever the church bell rang, Mr. Hovey marched the pupils to whatever service was going on. As my brother and I were not Catholics, we did not have to go, and instead played marbles until the pupils marched back.

The over-all scholastic advantages of these three years were of questionable value, but I did learn to speak Spanish and I learned about farming, horses, and nature. Perhaps the most important lessons I learned were the ones outside the classroom, for I really came to know and respect the culture of the Mexican-Americans and the San Felipe Indians.

My father was particularly interested in two mines, one being developed by a Mr. George Batchin, near Las Placitas, and the other the property of Mr. Ed McCarr, near San Pedro. Both of these old miners were guests at our house many times. Mr. Batchin wore a long, stringy mustache. My sister, when serving him coffee, would put it in a mustache cup, one with a partial covering which served as a shelf to rest his mustache, preventing the hairs from getting into the coffee. Mr. McCarr furnished amusement of a different kind. He was a large man with a flowing white beard, and while he ate, various bits fell and lodged in his whiskers. He corrected this by combing his beard with his fork, much to my sister's disgust.

During this time, my father also drilled two oil exploration wells near Tunque, fifteen miles northeast of Algodones, the site of the Tunque Indian ruins. This gave me many exciting experiences. Twelve-horse teams pulled massive wagons loaded with boilers and machinery up winding roads to the drill sites. The driver controlled the lead team with a "jerk line," accompanied by yells and imprecations which they seemed to understand. No doubt the derrick and drilling paraphernalia were crude compared to those used in later oil drilling, but it all seemed huge and marvelous to me. I also had the chance to explore the then undisturbed Tunque ruins, where I found many arrowheads and other artifacts.

The Rocky Mountain area is dotted with the remains of defunct mines, mills, and railroads, bearing witness to the enterprise and imagination of promoters of the late eighteen- and early nineteen-hundreds. They also had the genius for influencing would-be investors to part with their money. Those were the days when people paid for their successes and their mistakes, instead of asking the federal government to fund them. It was rumored that many could paper their homes with worthless stock certificates, but there were those who believed it better to be able to do this, and have a chance for riches and even fame, than to be able to paper them with tax receipts and not have a chance.

One such enterprise which came to my youthful attention was a proposed highline canal to take water from the Rio Grande at San Felipe Pueblo, some thirty miles north of Albuquerque, and make it available for irrigation for many miles down the valley. All through the years each community in the valley had had its own irrigation ditch called the *Acequia Madre* (mother ditch), originally dug and always maintained by the farmers who used its water. In each case, water was diverted from the river by a makeshift dam of rock and brush. During high water, the dams would wash out and would have to be replaced. One purpose of the proposed canal was to sell water to each irrigation system along its route, eliminating the need for the insecure diversions. It also made possible the reclamation of many hundreds of acres above the level of the valley floor. (This plan was essentially carried out by the Middle Rio Grande Conservancy District many years later.)

I came to know about this project because my oldest brother, John, worked on the survey crew laying out the canal route. I also saw it partially materialize by the construction of a rock and concrete diversion dam just south of San Felipe, as well as by a stretch of the canal reaching as far south as Algodones.

I suppose that hidden in some archive is a record of this ambitious and entirely practical enterprise—of the genius who conceived it and the plan for its completion. It might also show why it was abruptly abandoned after such an auspicious start. As a child, I felt the excitement of its prospects and suffered through the disappointment of its failure.

While we lived in Algodones, a Mr. Utley, from New York City, visited us and discussed the possibility of financing my father's smelter scheme. It was said he was a very rich man who had a seat on the Stock Exchange. The significance of a seat on the Stock Exchange was lost on a ten-year-old boy, but the amount of paper money he carried was not: bills of large and small denomination —the old authoritative-looking bills, three and one-half by eight inches with pictures of presidents on them. Paper money was not in general use in New Mexico in 1901, and these bills were a curiosity to us.

Mr. Utley was to return by train to New York, so we drove him to a flag station four miles north across the river from the San Felipe Pueblo. While waiting for the train, he saw an Indian woman sitting in the doorway of a parked boxcar and started to take her picture, but she covered her face with her shawl. He offered her a dollar bill to pose, but she refused, and even refused a five-dollar bill. My father told him to offer her a silver half-dollar. When he took the coin from his pocket, she smiled and posed for the picture very nicely.

For us, though, neither the mines, the smelter, nor the oil wells materialized into riches. But during this time we did make many friends that enriched our lives.

A family named Garcia lived at Angostura, just south of Algodones. Its members were all talented, the outstanding one being Tranquilino, a watchmaker and silversmith. His work required power, which he provided by building a most ingenious apparatus—a treadmill. It consisted of a large circular platform, so placed that when two mules walked up its slope, it turned, activating a rope pulley which turned a spindle at high speed. The spindle turned an arbor from which small pulleys turned grinding machines, buffers, drills, and all the other tools of his trade. It was all self-made, and a marvel to everyone who saw it. All traces of this assemblage of one man's genius have disappeared. It seems a pity it could not have been preserved.

To get to the San Felipe Indian Pueblo on the west side of the Rio Grande, one had to ford the river, or cross on a unique footbridge built by the Indians some sixty years before. In building the bridge, the Indians had woven huge willow baskets, placed them in the river about twelve feet apart, and filled them with rocks. These caissons were connected by two-by-twelve planks, making a precarious walkway across the river. I was told that prior to the availability of sawed planks hewn logs were used to span the distances between the baskets. These logs (and later the sawed planks), being hard to come by, were highly prized. When floodwaters threatened, a bridge brigade would run to the far end, pick up the last timber, and run with it to the west bank. Each successive timber was thus carried and piled above the high-water mark until the flood stage had passed, whereupon it was replaced in reverse order. In case a surprise flood carried away some timbers, the Indians hunted the river banks for miles to recover them.

As I remember, there were ten basket caissons. As they dammed the river considerably, the water level above them was raised, causing the flow between the baskets to be quite rapid. During flood time, the water would flow over the baskets, even at times dislodging some rock filling. In spite of this repeated punishment, the Indians claimed that in sixty years a basket had never washed out.

We always attended the Indian dances, as did many others. Wagon and buggy loads of visitors came, and sometimes Mr. Trimble's tallyho would bring a load from Albuquerque. Trains brought tourists from far-away places. Although the Indians were expert at crossing their bridge, to the uninitiated it was an alarming experience. The long boards bent under a person's weight and water rushed frighteningly near—only a foot or two below. A specially entertaining sight was to see lady tourists negotiate the bridge. Most were decked out as if for a festive occasion with huge hats, corseted waists, long flowing dresses, and high buttoned shoes. They were usually accompanied by a swain in a straw or derby hat and high starched collar. The swain would help his lady across by going ahead, extending a helping hand backwards, or ushering her ahead with a helping hand. Their double weight could cause the planks to bend lower, increasing both the actual and mental hazard. Their crossing would be accompanied by feminine squeals and shrieks as they crept gingerly along. The tourists came to see the show the Indians put on, but inadvertently furnished the Indians equal entertainment. Men, women, and children would gather on the bank to watch.

All this I saw and experienced, but was told what occurred afterwards. Progress marches on with time. The U.S. Indian Service decided sometime in the first years of the twentieth century that the Indians needed an up-to-date bridge—one for wagons and, eventually, cars. So a steel truss bridge was built some two hundred yards upstream from the old one. It was supported on concrete-filled steel piers and incorporated the latest features. And, in spite of the Indians' protests, the engineers tore out the basket caissons which had withstood sixty years of floods, stating it was necessary to do so to prevent impeding the river's flow.

The day of the dedication of the new bridge furnished the occasion for a gala celebration with speeches and ribbon cutting. It was said the governors of New Mexico and the pueblo, along with dignitaries of the Indian Service, riding in a handsome surrey pulled by beautiful white horses, led the procession across the bridge while a band played appropriate music. Afterwards everybody went home with feelings of a job well done—everybody, that is, but the Indians. They were suspicious and distrustful of this strange new bridge. The destruction of their old one, after it had served them so well, rankled in their bosoms.

That winter was an extremely severe one in the watershed country of the Rio Grande, with abnormal snowfall. When winter lifted and spring thaws came, the Rio Grande became a raging torrent, reaching peak flow in late May. The Indians saw the rising flood and they wondered. There were no boards to remove from their old bridge, as they had done for generations. They wondered what should be done to protect the monster that spanned their river, but the engineers reassured them. All would be well.

But all was not well! As the river approached its flood peak, the water whirled around the steel piers with ever greater suction force until, during a dark early morning in May, two of the piers' supports were literally lifted out of their sockets and dashed downstream with a great roar amid twisted girders and planks. At early dawn, the first Indian to see the catastrophe sounded the alarm and soon the bank was lined with men, women, and children. They were at first awestruck at what the Great Spirit had wrought, and then convulsed with mirth at the doings of the Great White Father and his minions.

Of course the federal government rebuilt the bridge, strong and durable, and today's Indians speed across it in pickups and heavy cars with never a thought for the old faithful bridge that had served their fathers so well. A few of the oldsters, however, still sit and ponder on the good old days when they skipped across the unstable planking or gathered on the bank to watch the big-hatted, small-waisted, blowing-skirted ladies mince across the planks with shrieks and squeals.

During the time I lived in Algodones, I came to appreciate the ways of the Indians, something I had not done in Albuquerque. When I first came there, Indians seemed to be everywhere—stolid, wrapped in blankets, and wearing moccasins. They intrigued yet frightened me. Most of my prior knowledge of Indians came from tales of their scalping depredations. After I had lived in Algodones those three years, I learned to accept them for what they are—thoroughbreds, dedicated and loyal to their code of standards, respectful of their elders and the disciplines imposed by their pueblo government.

My father had dealings with the San Felipe Indians and I visited their pueblo with him. I eventually made friends with Indian children and was invited to stay overnight with them. By day we played normal children's games with sticks, stones, cans, and small bows and arrows. I ate many meals with them, but the only foods I can remember were tamales, made in cornhusks, and a candy-like substance made by twisting muskmelon rinds into long, round shapes, which were then dried in the sun. What we ate were slices of this, which were much like baloney in appearance.

During the evenings, we sat on the floor and listened to tales related by the elders. They could speak some English, but spoke mostly in a slow, gutteral, simple Spanish that I could understand. Sometimes they would lapse into their language and the children would interpret for me. The tales were no doubt legends handed down from father to son. I can remember one in particular. It told of the San Felipes being attacked by another tribe and having to retreat to the high mesa back of the pueblo from where they could repulse the enemy. They had taken water with them, but it was soon used up; just when it appeared that thirst would force them to surrender, the medicine men held a dance beseeching the Great Father for help. A great white cloud appeared and a Being on a magnificent white horse descended to tell them to stand fast—that the heavens would bring them water. The rain came, giving them ample water, and the attackers saw the futility of further siege and departed.

At night I would sleep on a sheepskin on the floor with the rest of the family. After such a visit, my sister would give me a thorough treatment with blue ointment salve to rid me of any little creatures that might have been attracted to my heavy crop of red hair.

My father ran a store in Algodones to which the Indians brought corn and wheat to trade for such items as axes, shovels, harness parts, sugar, and so forth. They were barter transactions with little exchange of money. The Indians used a system of quantitative measurement, probably originally learned from the Spaniards. A box one-foot square and four-inches deep held what they called an *almor* of grain. Four *almores* made a *fanega,* somewhat over a bushel in their system. They valued their grain by these measurements, having little knowledge of, or faith in, pounds as registered by scales.

One time, after a group of Indians had been prodding around the store, an ax, a shovel, and other articles were missing. My father reported the theft to the governor of the pueblo and the articles were returned with no questions asked. The governor's discipline was absolute.

Each pueblo had, and still has, two types of festival occasions. One type was the public dances to which guests were invited without question, when the dance was given to invoke the assistance of the gods to bring rain, to assure successful crops, or (as at Christmas) to memorialize an occasion. The other type of festival was a secret affair, when only Indians of the particular pueblo could be present. These latter were a great mystery to us and still are to everyone but the Indians. On one such occasion, my sister was spending the night with Miss White, the resident government-school teacher in San Felipe. The Indians came to tell them to stay indoors during the night, and proceeded to cover all the windows with blankets. During the night, the two of them got little sleep—but repeatedly heard weird noises and thought they smelled burning flesh. On another occasion, my father was hauling a load of hay on a road that passed through the pueblo. He was met at the pueblo boundary by a delegation of Indians. They commandeered his team and wagon, told him to get home by going across the footbridge, and that his team and load would be delivered to him next day. And it was.

Even more spectacular to me than the dances were the annual rabbit hunts of the San Felipes. They were occasions of mass activity, part hunt and part picnic, participated in by men, women, and children. Coming in wagons and on horseback, but mostly on foot, they gathered in an area where scouts had reported the presence of rabbits. With no guns, they depended on throwing rocks, or cleverly fashioned clubs, to kill the game. In the hunt, those on horseback, equipped with clubs, would proceed in a company front. They were followed by a line of hunters on foot, equipped with stones and clubs. Next were men with shovels, and last came the wagons with the women.

Although it was called a rabbit hunt, they took any living thing they encountered—prairie dogs, gophers, lizards, snakes, and birds of any kind. When the horsemen spied a victim, they would run it down and attempt to club it while leaning down on a dead run. If the victim escaped this onslaught by doubling back, the foot hunters took up the chase. If it escaped into a hole, the shovel troops would dig it out. The only things that escaped were birds, and a surprising number of them were knocked down by accurately thrown stones or clubs.

When a kill was made, it was passed back to the women for dressing and then stored in a wagon. Certainly, very little was thrown away—skins, feathers, bones, and even entrails were kept for their various purposes. At midday, all would gather around the wagons for a feast.

One of these hunts would have been a horror for today's wildlife conservationists. But as the hunts were held only once a year, and never in the same area for two years in succession, the site seemed always to become repopulated in the meantime. At any rate, it is my recollection that there was much more ground cover and wildlife of every kind then than there is in those same areas today.

The Indians also furnished us great entertainment during their spring quest for fish. High water during the spring flooded areas of land adjacent to the river, leaving large ponds when the water subsided. These were usually filled with all manner of fish, frogs, and eels. Men, dressed only in G-strings, would seine the ponds, dumping the catch into barrels in the wagons. What was done later with the not-too-palatable-looking catch I never found out.

6

My sister and I moved back to Albuquerque in 1902, when I was about twelve, and took a house in the 1400 block on West Railroad Avenue. I had left school in mid-year of the fourth grade, and I returned at mid-year—to the same grade—three years later. As the Fourth Ward School was overcrowded, an annex school was opened in an old brick dwelling back of the Huning Castle, on either West Silver or West Gold Avenue, and I was assigned there. This was most fortunate for me, as the fourth and fifth grades in the annex were taught by Miss Elizabeth Willey, who had a profound influence on my life. I had forgotten my schooling and how to associate with Anglo boys—then being able to talk Spanish better than English. Miss Willey's sympathy and guidance helped to get me back into the stream of things with the least embarrassment. Children are sometimes cruel to one another, and I was a natural butt for their teasing and pranks. She straightened things out for me nicely, though. (We were fortunate years later, when Miss Willey ran a private school, to have our oldest son attend it.)

Some of those who attended the annex school were Kennedy

Strickler, Alvan Roberts, Gladys Mandell, Milton Ellsworth, and a boy whose last name was Henry. We had a happy time in the freedom allowed us during that school half-year. When the river reached flood stage, the school was surrounded by water with only a raised dirt path leading to town, and two paths leading to the boys' and girls' privies back of the school. This created a feeling of cozy excitement.

Many of our teachers had a lasting influence on our lives: Mr. C. Roy Kiger, Miss Eva W. Bowers, and Mr. J. Ross McCollum at the Fourth Ward School. (Mr. McCollum, whom I valued as a lifelong friend, became a noted state educator.) At mid-year, our sixth grade was moved to the Central School at the corner of Third Street and Lead Avenue, where Miss Mabel Tracy taught us. (She later married Jerry Haggard, who worked in the State National Bank.) Miss Mary L. Hartig taught us in the seventh grade. As she was of German parentage, she induced many of us to take first-year German, a great help in my engineering courses in later years. In the eighth grade, I was fortunate in having the dean of teachers of those times, Mrs. Ella La Bar. Before leaving the subject of grade-school teachers, I should mention Miss Mabel I. Fitch. She was a circulating teacher of art and music, dividing her time among the four grade schools. She had the genius to instill in her pupils a love of music and drawing—no mean accomplishment, considering our ages. She taught us "tricks" in drawing which I have used all my life.

The heavenly reward that I hope is accorded teachers may have been the only recognition many of the early ones received. Too often they were unappreciated and woefully underpaid—in some cases only in a scrip, which was a sort of official IOU called county warrants. The scrip could be used to purchase things in the stores, but only at a terrific discount. It is a sad commentary on a society that it paid its political officeholders—the sheriff, the county clerk, the assessor—in money; but the teachers, whose value to society exceeded all the rest put together, got IOUs. One sees the same tendency today when people vote against school bonds and then complain about the inadequacy of the school system.

Our next move was to the 900 block on North First Street. This move opened up new experiences and contacts for me, including the meeting of my lifelong friend, Jack Lapraik. Most of my experiences until after we graduated from the University were shared with him. The Continental Oil Company storage yard was a block north of our house; Lemp's Brewery distributing warehouse was across First Street next to the railroad tracks; Ernest Hall lived across the street; the Lapraiks, the V. P. Edies, the Hales, and Chief Thomas McMillin lived back of us on Second Street.

Ralph Damiano ran the Lemp's warehouse and distributed kegs of beer daily in a sharp-looking wagon, pulled by a pair of beautiful black horses. I made friends with Ralph, and he often took me on his rounds to saloons located all over town. Perhaps this was not the best recreational pursuit for a twelve-year-old boy, but I enjoyed it and became acquainted with more of the town.

I had much innocent fun with the friends I made during this period. We, like the other kids in town, played at such pastimes as "shoot the Indians," an early version of cops and robbers, and "duck on rock," where one round rock was placed on top of another and the game was to knock it off with another rock from thirty feet away. We also spent many hours at marbles, tops, baseball, football, and shinny. There were no playgrounds, or splendid equipment, and no play supervisors—just spontaneous fun in any vacant lot. I never understood how the "seasons" for children's sports came about. A season for marbles, and kids all over town were playing marbles. It seemed to start simultaneously and end as abruptly. Then might come top season, when everyone was spinning tops. Tops might give way to shinny (a forerunner to hockey) and it in turn to run-sheep-run, and so on. It was as though some Master Coxswain called the orders and all complied. (Today they might call it a result of extrasensory perception.) The merchants, too, seemed to get the signals. Marble season—and the marbles were taken out of storage and displayed attractively. Top season—and the show windows would be resplendent with all kinds and colors of tops.

We made sleds and when it snowed hooked rides back of buggies and wagons. This, incidentally, was a cute trick. We would run after a vehicle and slip the rope, which was attached to the sled, over the vehicle's rear axle and, holding the rope, lie down on the sled to be pulled along through the snow and slush. If a driver discovered us, he would sometimes smile and nod, sometimes whip up his horse to give us a faster ride, or sometimes object to the prank and whip us off, which we complied with by merely turning the rope loose.

An important industrial enterprise was the wool scouring mill located east of the tracks on Mountain Road where the Springer Transfer Company's main office was later built. The mill occupied a huge, two-story black frame building. Each year large sacks of wool were brought from the shearing pens, heavy with grease, dirty, and full of burrs and sticks. After having been run through the scouring process, it came out wonderfully white and fluffy, ready for the looms. Some weaving was done on the second floor of the building, but most of the wool was baled and shipped to the New England states, where the nation's weaving was done.

The plant was run by a Mr. J. H. Bearrup, whose home was situated in an entire city block and surrounded by a high board fence. McClellan Park on North Fourth Street now occupies this block. The home was surrounded by a fine orchard, and one of our extracurricular activities was to raid this orchard. Mr. Bearrup had developed an effective deterrent to these youthful depredations. He loaded shotgun shells with fine salt and would pepper (excuse the pun) the miscreants' behinds with this saline charge. I found one such experience discouraging to further forays.

Mr. Bearrup had two sons. Perhaps prompted by a burst of patriotism, he named one of them Bernalillo. The euphony of the name Bernalillo Bearrup appealed to our sense of humor.

Coal and wood were the only available sources of fuel for cooking and heating. Coal, mined near Gallup and Madrid, was brought in railroad coal cars and sold by the Hahn Coal Company and others. Wood was principally supplied by Mexican-Americans who lived in the mountains and Tijeras Canyon. It was a common sight to see these wood-haulers trailing over the mesa roads and down Railroad Avenue, with scrawny teams, pulling rickety wagons loaded with an unstable-looking stack of juniper and piñon logs. The driver, and sometimes his wife or child, would be perched precariously on top. They sold their wood to wood yards, took their money and stocked up with items from the stores, and with their new load tied uncertainly on the framework of the wagon, made the long trek across the mesa to the mountains. To furnish water to the wood-haulers, as well as to other drivers and horses and animals, the city had placed a grand-looking granite drinking fountain and horse trough in the middle of the intersection of Broadway and Railroad Avenue. An unplanned by-product of this wood hauling was transportation to town for students at the University. Even before I entered the University, I remember seeing boys, and girls too, from the University perched atop a loaded wood wagon as it jostled down the rough roadway of Railroad Avenue.

In the Continental Oil Company yard, there were huge tanks for storing kerosene (we called it coal oil) and smaller tanks for storing naphtha and gasoline. One day about noon the plant caught

fire, and that was the most spectacular and satisfactory fire of all. As a tank got hot, it would blow the safety plug on top and a column of flame would shoot in the air hundreds of feet. A kerosene tank wagon, which held about a thousand gallons, was evidently built of heavier metal than the other tanks, because it withstood the heat the longest. But when it did go, it shot the highest of all. From our house a block away we had a premium viewing position, but at times we wondered if our home might catch from the extreme heat. The fire burned into the night—when it was the most spectacular. All the tanks finally exploded, so we were witness to a super Fourth-of-July-style spectacle. The next morning all that remained was a mass of smoldering debris.

The route of the Santa Fe Railroad followed the bed of a slough from the river, which hugged the sand hills bordering the valley to the east. To prevent the Rio Grande from overflowing into its old slough channel, the company built a dike along the river bank north of Alameda. The dike served very well for many years except when abnormally high floods occurred. I can remember several occasions when this happened—a crisis situation then developed which affected the whole New Town community. The fire siren sounded, the curfew bell rang, and the shop's whistle blew and blew. These were the accepted signals for community action and, whether it was night or day, volunteers from all walks of life rushed in wagons, in buggies, on horseback, and even in Mr. Trimble's tallyho, to the scene of the threatened break to fill and place bags of sand, cut brush, or do whatever was necessary to reinforce the dike.

When we were living on North First Street, the dike broke through in spite of all these efforts. The water followed its time-accustomed route and ran down the west side of the railroad borrow pit. By dint of tremendous labor with teams and scrapers and dump wagons, a temporary dike was thrown up south of Mountain Road to drain the water west to the river.

We boys "borrowed" lumber from a nearby construction project and built a boat with which, for a nickel, we proposed to ferry people from the railroad track to the raised boardwalk on the west side of First Street. Being inexperienced at boat building, we made one serious mistake. We nailed the bottom boards on to the side boards from below so that as we trod on the bottom boards, they were continually loosened. This caused leaking, and the more we

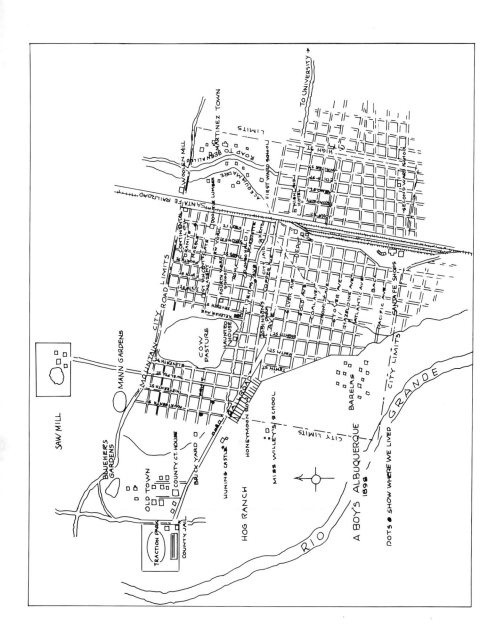

A BOY'S ALBUQUERQUE
1898

DOTS ● SHOW WHERE WE LIVED

1. *Looking east on Railroad (Central) Avenue, ca. 1900.*

2. *Looking east from Fifth and Gold, ca. 1905.*

3. *Hunting party in front of the White Elephant Saloon, 1900.*

4. *A streetcar in 1900.*

5. *Interior of the Commercial Club, mid-1890s.*

6. *Fourth Ward School, mid-1890s.*

7. *Class portrait, Fourth Ward School, 1910.*

8. *St. Vincent's Girls School, ca. 1900.*

9. *Kenneth Balcomb (left) and Paul Ellis in front of the old blacksmith's shop on the Ellis Ranch, ca. 1900.*

10. *Four generations of Ellises, 1897.*

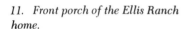

11. *Front porch of the Ellis Ranch home.*

12.   U.S. Post Office, 1890s.

13.   Corner of Second and Silver, with the Post Office on the left, ca. 1900.

14. *Washburn clothier, 1910.*

15. *Drygoods and clothing store of the Mandell Brothers, mid-1890s.*

16. Zeiger's Cafe, ca. 1895.

17. Alvarado Hotel Dining Room, 1908.

18. *Decorations for the welcoming of President Theodore Roosevelt in 1904 Second and Railroad (Central).*

19. *Col. D. K. B. Sellers (left) with Chief of Police Thomas McMillin, 1912.*

20. *Albuquerque Wool Scouring Mill, c. 1900.*

21. *Wool wagons at 400 Railroad (Central) Avenue, mid-1890s.*

22. *American Lumber Company, ca. 1900.*

23. *Robinson Park bandstand, 1900.*

24. *Laying the cornerstone of Temple Albert Synagogue at Seventh and Gold, 1899.*

25. Bernalillo County Court House, 1908.

26. Ed Harsch, of Coyote Water fame, in his Fergusson Hook and Ladder Company uniform, 1900.

27. Judging committee of the New Mexico Territorial Fair, ca. 1900.

28. *Railroad car with banner announcing the Territorial Fair, ca. 1900.*

29. *Carnival week of 1904, with tents between Second and Third streets on Railroad (Central) Avenue.*

30. *University of New Mexico football team, 1914. Kenneth Balcomb (sixth from right) played right halfback and fullback.*

31. *Albuquerque Baseball Team, ca. 1900.*

32. *Looking south on Second Street from Central, with O'Rielly's drugstore on the right, 1908.*

33. *University of New Mexico, ca. 1900.*

moved around the more it leaked, necessitating continual bailing. This hampered our ferry operation seriously. The weight of an added person caused more leaking, and all hands, including the passenger, had to bail madly to prevent the boat from sinking in midstream.

We decided to quit carrying big people and to confine our venture to giving little kids a ride for a nickel. One such prospective customer was George Doolittle, son of George Doolittle, who ran the Albuquerque Lumber Yard. He did not have a nickel, so we suggested he run home and get one, but instead of a nickel, he brought a sack of cookies which he offered as fare, and which we accepted. As he climbed in, he was given a can with which to bail, which he did valiantly. In later years, George would recall this experience and complain that he not only had to pay for his ride, but had to work for it too.

Our venture was not a financial success, but I can remember having great fun and getting gloriously muddy and wet.

Establishment of the American Lumber Company seemed to play an important role in our young lives as it did, of course, in the economy of the town. It was a spectacular operation. Great train loads of beautiful logs came in from distant places called Zuñi, Grants, and McGaffey, and they were dumped with a great splash into a large pond that had been scooped out of a field. Men with spiked boots jumped nimbly from log to floating log, maneuvering them into a place where huge grappling claws lifted and turned them like match sticks. Finally they would ascend on an endless chain, to be fed onto a carriage that raced back and forth at the will of a superman called a sawyer. The sawyer sat high in a windowed cubicle and exercised his will by pulling cranks and pushing buttons. As the carriage raced forward, it would project the log into a vicious-looking saw that ripped through it from end to end, cutting a neat board. In this manner, it would be rushed back and forth until the entire log had been reduced to boards. As the boards fell away from the carriage, they were in turn grappled and shoved over a series of moving belts, while another superman in another high cubicle pulled levers and pushed buttons to activate saws that trimmed the boards to desired widths and lengths. These operations took place in a riot of sound, but with a precision that was fascinating. We boys stood by the hour watching it.

Those were the days before cartons, made from corrugated paper, were designed to package anything from a pencil to a refrigerator. Wooden boxes of all shapes and sizes were used to contain things, and a box factory was a very important part of the mill enterprise. It was also important to us boys as, during vacation time, many were employed in the box factory to do various jobs at ten cents an hour for a ten-hour day. Those who got these jobs were looked upon with considerable envy.

The whole mill operation took place in an extensive fenced area northwest of town, reached by an extension of North Twelfth Street and by a spur track from the railroad. The area was a beehive of activity in many spacious, low frame buildings housing the various operations. A screened cone rose high in the air and into it an inclined belt continually dumped sawdust and trash pieces. The resultant fire burned day and night, emitting a rolling volume of white smoke. One could buy a load of kindling for a dollar. It made excellent firewood, but also furnished delightful little boards with which a boy could fashion things.

Although we boys would refer to a dilapidated bicycle, or any rickety conveyance, as an "ice wagon," the comparison was unrealistic. Those were the days before ice-making machines, miniaturized to fit into home refrigerators, were standard equipment. Instead of these marvels for food preservation, people had insulated iceboxes, which came in sizes varying from small ones to hold a ten-pound chunk of ice, up to splendid walk-in affairs that held several hundred-pound cakes. It was the job of the iceman to circulate about town and keep these boxes supplied with ice. The wagon he used to haul the ice was the sturdiest vehicle on the streets—covered, well insulated, and pulled by a powerful team of horses. We looked forward to the iceman's visit in the neighborhood. He had to saw the hundred-pound cakes into sizes to fit the various boxes, and there were always delicious chunks to be had for sucking.

The principal source of ice was the Diamond Ice Company, located along a spur track in the north part of town. We would go there to watch the marvelous process by which steel tanks of fresh water, after being immersed in a huge tank of brine for a few hours, would be lifted out and emptied of a crystal-clear, four-hundred-

pound block of ice. The means by which the temperature of the brine was reduced below the freezing point of fresh water, and why the brine did not freeze, was explained to us, but always remained a thing of mystery, as does the miniaturized version in our deep freezer today.

It was a spectacular show to see the icing of refrigerated freight cars which carried perishables. The train of cars would be run onto the siding next to the icehouse; one-hundred-pound cakes of ice were run along an elevated track to the top of the first car and along it to the ice chamber at each end. Each car was thus iced as the train was moved forward. The speed and accuracy were fascinating.

Something happened about this time that struck terror into all of us. A man who ran a wood and coal yard in the neighborhood went berserk. He was evidently quite liberal in extending credit to his customers, and it was his inability to collect what was owed him that caused his mental aberration. He became so upset he undertook to collect from his debtors by threatening to kill them with an ax. It became so serious that it was necessary to lock him up in the mental hospital at Las Vegas.

The very fact that an insane man was going about threatening to kill people with an ax was enough to strike terror into a boy. But what made it worse for me was that my father had been one of his customers, had not paid his bill, and was, therefore, one of the objects of the ax forays. I can remember the relief we felt when the man was confined in Las Vegas, but also the increased fear when it was announced that he had escaped and was even more determined to wreak vengeance on those who had done him wrong. Until he had been recaptured and again incarcerated, we locked all the doors, pulled down the blinds, and listened with bated breath whenever we heard a sound outside the house.

7

For political and school purposes, Albuquerque was divided into four wards, separated north from south by Railroad Avenue, and east from west by the railroad tracks. The First Ward was to the northeast, the Second Ward to the southeast, the Third Ward to the southwest, and the Fourth Ward to the northwest. Each had a two-story red brick school building that appeared to have been built from the same set of plans; each had grades one through six, and about the same organization of teacher staff. In the eyes of the pupils, however, that was where the similarity ended. The pupils of each were convinced that the pupils of the other schools were low characters, capable of any sort of meanness, and hence were fair game when caught at a disadvantage. An inter-school athletic contest was apt to end in an exchange of fisticuffs, leaving forever unsettled which team was the better in play.

Being of the Fourth Ward, we felt ourselves to be comparative gentlemen. We rated the others in the following order: first, the First Ward, because young "Doc" Cornish went there and was a stellar athlete; next, the Second Ward, which really didn't amount

59

to much anyway; and last, the Third Ward, where, in our opinion, was concentrated the worst assortment of brigands in town.

These animosities were somewhat like those between fraternity members in a university—potent and real at the time, but because of no sound substance, transitory, and erased entirely as we grew older and assumed friendships with our former archenemies.

Knowledge of the corporate limits of New Town, of Albuquerque, and of its surrounding country came to me slowly as I grew older and traveled farther afield. Cromwell Avenue was the town's southern limit, Fourteenth Street the western boundary, Mountain Road the north limit, and High Street the limit to the east. In 1898, even within these restricted limits, there were large vacant areas, such as the cattle pasture west of Keleher Avenue. These filled up as the population increased. Lovely homes were built on the streets facing Robinson Park; attractive bungalows sprang up on "Honeymoon Row" (along the south side of Railroad Avenue between Eighth and Fourteenth streets). Later the cattle pasture gave way to Luna Park, along North Ninth, Tenth, and Eleventh streets.

Above High Street, only a few houses existed as far as the University, and there was nothing beyond. An old, weather-beaten, yellow frame house was perched on a hill just south of Railroad Avenue at Elm Street, only a block east of High Street. The story was that the house had been built on a 160-acre homestead. Eventually the house was abandoned, but it endured and suffered —its windows gaping holes, the doors broken, and great holes in the roof where shingles had blown off.

In 1912, when I was on the University football team, we had been unable to win a game. When we played out of town, we traveled by train and we would have to walk down sandy Railroad Avenue to the depot, lugging our football paraphernalia. Each time, as we passed the old frame house, our coach, Ralph Hutchinson, would say, "Well, boys, if we beat this team, we will burn down the old frame house when we get back." Finally we won a game, and the excitement on the return trip rose to a high pitch in anticipation of burning the old house. We arrived after dark, and all rushed up the hill to start the blaze, only to find the house was gone. It had been moved away in our absence.

The extension of Railroad Avenue east of High Street became a wavering sandy lane as far as the University; from there a wagon road wound uncertainly till it entered Tijeras Canyon, which in

Spanish means scissors, so called because it branches at its upper end into two canyons—Tijeras and Cedro. On its way to the canyon it passed an adobe and rock structure that had the reputation of harboring ladies of questionable reputation, but displayed the innocent sign "Tea and Cakes." At the mouth of the canyon was a structure known as Trimble's Rock House, which was vacant and always seemed mysterious to us. A short way into the canyon was a large spread in a park-like setting known as Selva's. Beyond that was a series of small Mexican villages.

The city water reservoir was then, as now, located at Yale Avenue, but was much smaller. In spite of the high board fence that surrounded it, it was a temptation for small folk to take a dip in the clear water destined for human consumption.

Owing to the then-clear atmosphere, the Sandia Mountains seemed much closer than they do now. We were brought up on the story of the Easterner who, when his way was blocked by a narrow irrigation ditch, balked at jumping it. When asked why he didn't leap across, he said, "No sir. I was fooled by thinking I could walk the short distance to the mountains before breakfast only to find they are eight miles away. This ditch is probably twice as wide as it appears."

Perhaps the very young are insensitive to the miseries of others. At any rate, I cannot remember knowing that Albuquerque was a health resort—that all around me were victims of the dread malady of tuberculosis. We grew up in the environment of consumptives, and accepted it as we did all that came within our purview. It was not until I had advanced into my teens that I became conscious that our town was a health resort, and I was a young man before I realized there was a period in the history of Albuquerque when both the dollars imported by health seekers and the payroll of the Santa Fe Railroad had sustained the economy of the town.

Before the discovery of the miracle drugs, eastern doctors recommended the dry climate of the Southwest for the cure for tuberculosis, and health seekers by the thousands came to Albuquerque—to fill sanatoriums, rooming houses, homes, and even to live in tents. One eminent tuberculosis specialist was heard to remark that if a medication for the cure for tuberculosis was ever discovered, it would ruin Albuquerque. This dire prediction did not materialize, but it did indicate how much the town had come to depend on those so unfortunately afflicted. Many did not get well, of course, but the marvel is that so many did. It turned out that the lasting benefit to the city was not the dollars that were imported by the health seekers, but the caliber of citizens that came with this influx. We came to have professional men and women—doctors, lawyers, teachers, scientists, writers, newspaper men—whose talents greatly exceeded what normally might have been expected in a small western town. High-caliber people in all walks of life came and got well and prospered—and Albuquerque prospered because of them.

Before victrolas, radios, and television were perfected, music-hungry people had principally to rely on home talents to satisfy their cravings: in musicals, band concerts, glee clubs, and orchestras. Each Sunday night during warm weather band concerts were held at Robinson Park, then the only public greensward and bandstand in town. Hundreds of people would occupy park benches, sit in chairs they brought, or stroll around visiting and enjoying the music. We boys enjoyed these occasions, too, but I am afraid not so much for the music as the opportunity to play and frolic.

A very worthwhile service to the community was rendered by the Learnard and Lindemann Music Store on West Gold Avenue. They organized young folk's orchestras and bands and coached the members. No doubt the direct purpose in this was to sell musical instruments, but I am sure men like Elmer Reihl, Don Wilson, Charlie Clark, and many others who went through this training would vouch for their having performed a civic service that transcended the profit motive.

Mr. Ed B. Harsch, who lived on South Broadway and had his place of business on South First, antedated Coca Cola, Pepsi Cola, and 7UP by a quarter of a century. Instead of concocting his soft drinks from herbs in artificially carbonated water, he merely backed a tank wagon to a faucet which ran from a spring in Coyote Canyon, filled the tank, hauled it to his place of business, put it in bottles, and sold it as Coyote Water. It was the most popular drink of the era. It had a tangy taste and a fizzy effervescence that tingled one's nostrils while drinking it. The spring was about five miles into Coyote Canyon, which is the first sizable one south of Tijeras Canyon. We boys would hike into the canyon and be famished by the time we reached the spring. Mr. Harsch, or some kindly soul, had conveniently chained a tin drinking cup to a rock, and with it

we would drink our fill of the pungent liquid. (Unfortunately, Coyote Spring is now within the Sandia Base domain and off limits to anyone not carrying a clearance card.)

The recreation areas for Albuquerque—where folks went to escape summer heat, to picnic, or to celebrate the Fourth of July—had to be close by because of slow transportation. The attractive Jemez and Upper Pecos areas were delightful and had good fishing, but to get to either place was a hard, two-day trip by team and wagon, with all equipment and food, and only to be undertaken for long stays. Bear Canyon or Whitcomb Springs could be negotiated in a one-day round trip. Each had pure, cold running water, free from pollution, and pine trees and undergrowth that furnished wonderful camping places. On the Fourth of July, it seemed that half the town's population would go to the mountains

—on foot, on horseback, by buggy and wagon, and even in Mr. Trimble's tallyho. The winding, sandy roads would be dotted with moving humanity, going up in the morning and returning in the evening, usually all by daylight, as there were no headlights to light the way for the conveyances.

Bear Canyon was especially popular as it was the closest. Along the lower stretches of the live stream were cottonwoods, box elders, piñon, and cedar, while farther up were pines and quaking aspen. Perishables were kept cool in the stream. The two or three waterfalls in the stream were everyone's delight. To us children, these were wonderful times, even if we had to walk to get there.

Santa Fe, too, was a delightful place to spend a holiday. It offered a wonderful climate, the softest of water, and a citizenry that defied description in its heterogeneity. Even in the horse-and-buggy days, when the trip to Santa Fe was perforce by rail, it was a most tempting weekend trip for Albuquerqueans. They went main line Santa Fe Railroad to Lamy, where lunch could be had at an adorable little Harvey House, then by spur railroad over a winding route, on a jerky train pulled by a belching locomotive, up the additional 1500 feet in elevation to the City of Santa Fe station. (Here, if one wished to go farther afield, he could entrain on a Denver and Rio Grande narrow-gauge railroad to Antonito, Colorado.) Of course, everyone was well aware that the Santa Fe police traveled in pairs, and provided a considerable source of the city's revenue by arresting Albuquerqueans who might have tippled too much and become boisterous. But that was all a part of a Santa Fe holiday.

Rivalry between Santa Fe, the territorial capital city, and Albuquerque, the budding metropolis, was keen but friendly, even though there was a latent fear in Santa Fe that Albuquerque would like to steal the capitol the way they accused it of stealing the university. This unfounded claim arose because a private institution called the University of New Mexico had been started in Santa Fe in 1881. The Territorial Legislature of 1889, however, provided for the establishment of a state-supported University of New Mexico at Albuquerque. Probably no covetous intent to steal the capitol ever existed. After all, what was more appropriate than for Santa Fe, the capital of the territory under the flags of Spain and Mexico, to remain the capital under the Stars and Stripes?

Old Town Albuquerque had been flooded with wave after wave of people by 1880, when the Santa Fe Railroad laid its steel rails down the valley. For two-and-a-half centuries the tide of seekers for gold along with farmers and soldiers—mostly Spanish and Mexican—had ebbed and flowed, always leaving a residue of settlers in the adobe village on the banks of the Rio Grande. By 1900, the vigorous original settlers had, of course, all passed to their Maker, but the fourth and fifth generation descendants remained. They were principally of one ethnic group and one religious persuasion; as heirs to stable cultural patterns and settled habits, they devoted themselves to the preservation of this inheritance with little desire for change.

By contrast, the adventurers who had followed the railroad in its "opening of the West" and had settled in New Town Albuquerque were very active at the turn of the century—energetic, effective manpower in the community. Also, the new pioneers were of every race, creed, and color—a veritable melting pot of English, Spanish, Mexican, German, Italian, even a few Chinese and blacks, and Protestants, Catholics, and Jews. This mixture of pioneering stock seemed to result in a competitive spirit and an entrepreneurial vigor in the new community, similar to that of other western towns and of the nation as a whole.

Perhaps my evaluations of the business and civic contributions of turn-of-the-century Albuquerqueans were the result of a child's view of the adult world, but I remember men and women who seemed to me to stand out as superior people: P. F. McCanna the insurance man; O. A. Matson, who ran a stationery store; Sam Vann the jeweler; Louis Ilfeld, who dealt in sheep and wool; A. B. McMillen the attorney; Dr. P. G. Cornish; J. C. Baldridge; Dr. John F. Pearce; O. N. Marron the attorney and his partner, Mr. Francis E. Wood; Mrs. Margaret Medler the real-estate lady; the Kelehers; Tom and Frank Hubbell; and Dr. Walter G. Hope and his lovely and gracious wife. Such people made a great impression on me from my distant point of observation, and I am sure they appeared to me so superior because they were so distinguished in the town.

There were wonderful Jewish families of whom I can remember the Lewinsons, Weinmans, Grunsfelds, Ilfelds, Weillers, Maharams, and Nordhauses. Equally prominent were such Italian families as the Bachechis, Palladinos, Giacomellis, Matteuccis, Badaraccos, and Giomis, to name a few. There were many descendants of the original Spanish families in New Mexico: the Oteros, Yrisarris, Chaveses, Bacas, Pereas—and the list could go on and on. All these people and others of their contemporaries seemed to me to be big, strong people, and I am sure they were instrumental in forming the original fabric of a town that has had such phenomenal success.

Years after my youthful Albuquerque experiences, I read the following in Harry Golden's small book, *For Two Cents Plain:* "The saloonkeepers represented the backbone of organized charity in the days before community chests and charity foundations. The saloon-keeper was not only the easiest touch, but his establishment was the first call the committee made when something was needed in the neighborhood, like giving someone a decent funeral, or putting up bail for a wayward boy."

Mr. Golden was talking of conditions in his beloved Brooklyn neighborhood, but he also described what went on in all small towns in the West during the first few years of this century. When Dan Padilla was trying to organize a baseball team, the Albuquerque Grays, it was said it took him only half a day to raise the necessary $15,000 by visiting the saloons along Railroad Avenue. When uniforms for the town band were needed, when it was decided to send the Learnard and Lindemann Music Store band on a state tour, or when funds were needed to help the family of a policeman killed in the line of duty, the saloonkeepers and their ever-present patrons responded generously.

The sums may seem small in comparison with today's standards, but such as they were, they were freely offered. And, though the sums were small they represented strong purchasing power when a loaf of bread or a good cigar cost only five cents, newspapers were two cents, the best cuts of steak were fifteen cents a pound, and, with the purchase of a large mug of beer in a saloon, one got for free a turkey, chicken, or ham sandwich. If one bought a suit of clothes for twenty dollars, he received a free belt, or with a two-dollar shirt a present of a tie.

Easy money and generous gratuities prevailed in spite of low wages—ten cents an hour for a laborer, while the best carpenter was paid only four dollars for a ten-hour day. A $12,000 home was a mansion and $100,000 was a fortune. Poverty existed, to be sure, but I wonder whether it was proportionately any more prevalent than it is today after five decades of attempts to redistribute the wealth.

In this developing era, people were looking to the west for golden opportunities and always expecting good results. Around the turn of the century, my brother John worked on a survey crew laying out the route of a railroad being built in the Estancia valley. There was much big talk about this. A branch line was to run into Albuquerque through the Tijeras Canyon, to be called the Albuquerque Eastern. (Grades for it were partially constructed through the canyon and out onto the mesa east of town.)

At that time the Estancia valley furnished a vast and profitable open sheep range where legendary sheep men ran large flocks—a Scot, William McIntosh; an Irishman named Michael Timothy Moriarty; the J. A. Lapraiks, Stuarts, and others. Estancia (Spanish for *resting place*) was a spot where cottonwood trees for shade and water for the horses had provided a stopping place for travelers hauling salt from the salt lakes, which are east of the present town of Willard, to the towns in the Rio Grande valley. Mr. McIntosh was a picturesque character. A large man with a flowing red beard, he would frequently throw a big party in Albuquerque, with drinking, eating, dancing, and a gift of a piano to the lady winner of some sort of contest.

After the completion of the New Mexico Central Railroad, real-estate boomers started a land sale in the Estancia valley, bringing train loads of prospects from the Middle West and East to buy cheap land where the soil was fertile (true), the climate was superb (true), and where there was available an abundance of subsurface water (untrue). The towns of Stanley, Moriarty, McIntosh, and Estancia were laid out, lots were sold, and each became a boom town with everyone happy and excited over the prospects in this Golden Valley.

And then the bubble burst! Slowly, but surely, the purchasers of land learned that water in sufficient quantities for irrigation of farm land was not to be had, and for the next twenty years disheartened, half-starved, and hopeless families came out of the Estancia valley with the remnants of their worldly goods piled high on decrepit wagons pulled by emaciated horses.

The land boom also wrecked the sheep men who had enjoyed the largesse of grasses in the valley. The first act of the would-be farmers was to fence, the next was to plow. The openness of the range was destroyed along with the climax grasses.

In those days there were apparently no laws to prevent such misrepresentation of land conditions and the swindling of gullible purchasers.

8

MOST OF OUR YOUTHFUL PLEASURES in Albuquerque resulted from our being surrounded with nature's opportunities for amusement and interest: vacant land, bare hills, unpolluted streams, and abundant wildlife. What seemed our most exciting sources of pleasure, however, were wholly man-assembled—the arrival of a circus and the holding of the annual territorial fair. These were anticipated for a whole year, and realization always seemed better than anticipation.

I can remember the circus as being the Barnum and Bailey extravaganza. It would be set up in an area later called Hopewell Field, just east of the railroad tracks on Tijeras Avenue. All year long this area was covered with weeds and trash until, presto, on the given morning it would blossom into a city of tents and billboard adornment, with sawdust spread to cover the dust and stubble. The coming of the circus was well heralded for weeks in advance by the newspapers and by billboards and handbills illustrating ferocious tigers or enormous elephants. Our excitement mounted as the advertising became more eloquent.

About midnight before the day of the performance the train bearing the whole circus would slide onto a siding and pandemonium would break loose. Kerosene torches lighted up the whole area, and ramps were placed at each end of the train to allow debarking of the wagons carrying cages and equipment. First to be unloaded were the elephants and huge horses. They were hitched to the wagons to pull them along the train, down the ramps, and to the circus grounds. Although there seemed to be great confusion in the dark, with much shouting and clamor, everything proceeded with remarkable organization. All knew their jobs and did them.

The elephants were not given water during their long train ride, and they were desperately thirsty on arrival. We were eager to volunteer to carry water to them, as this was proverbially a source of free passes to the performance.

The magic of unloading and the miracle of raising the huge tents were sources of wonderment to us. We never fathomed the mysterious process by which huge, awkward, billowing canvasses would suddenly rise into the night air and take shape as graceful arenas. Here again pandemonium seemed to reign, with flickering, smoking torches, the shouts of many voices, and men running everywhere; but the marvel of organization and the familiarity with tasks performed repeatedly allowed for an orderly progress that was little short of miraculous.

By 10:00 A.M., the tents were up, the bleachers in place, and all would be lined up for the parade. The route of the parade seemed always to go west on Tijeras to Eighth, south on Eighth to Gold, east on Gold to Sixth, then north to Railroad Avenue, whence it turned east to Broadway and then back to the circus grounds. They were splendid parades. First would come a shiny carriage bearing the mayor and the head man of the circus (Mr. Barnum or Mr. Bailey, we presumed). Then would come the fire department equipment, the fire engine belching smoke; then the circus band, resplendent in red uniforms with brass braid and buttons and huge "beefeater hats." The elephants would come in single file, the largest one first, followed by the smaller ones, each one's trunk holding to the tail of the one in front. The baby would be last, taking a running step to keep up. Cages of animals would follow, with the clowns bringing up the end.

There was always an afternoon and a night performance. If we had tickets from carrying water to the elephants, we preferred the afternoon performance. Tickets were sold from a ticket wagon placed in the sawdust outside the first tent. Sometimes when we had not earned a ticket by watering the elephants, we stood around looking very anxious and hoping some good samaritan would buy us a ticket. When all these methods failed and we were forced to get in by other means, we preferred to go at night when the cover of darkness made it easier to sneak in. Our tried and true method was to hide outside the main tent until the guard had passed on his beat and then slip under the canvas. We would find ourselves in a dark cavern-like place under the bleachers, with hundreds of legs dangling down. Our technique was then very simple. We would start tapping men's legs, and sure enough before long, a hand would reach down to pull one of us up to a seat alongside our benefactor.

Although I hope I still have a residue of youth in my makeup, I am not prompted to see a circus again. I am sure the routine is about the same, with electric lights supplanting torches, and trucks and tractors replacing horsepower (and the train). I'm sure, also, that the shapely aerial artists are still admired as of yore, the horseback riders still flip from horse to horse as if suspended like

marionettes, the elephants on command still sit on tubs, or mount their forefeet on each other's rumps, and the clowns still go through their hilarious antics. Rather than go to a circus now and chance disillusionment, I prefer to relive the memories of these boyhood impressions. The imperceptible process of aging reaches a point that, when passed, forbids return.

The annual territorial fair, although much less pretentious than today's fairs, was wonderful to young folks. Perhaps its relative simplicity made the fair more enjoyable for us. The fairgrounds, known as Traction Park, began where Railroad Avenue reached Old Town Boulevard. To the left of the great gate was the ticket window, and to the left of that was the County Jail, a grim reminder to behave. To the right of the entrance were the exhibition buildings. The high board fence surrounding the fair-grounds reached almost to the river to the west. The grandstand stood along the south side, center to the half-mile racetrack which circled the field inside the fence. The area within the racetrack held a baseball diamond and room for other activities.

Seepage from the river during peak flows often caused wet spots on the ground, and someone with a diabolical mind would spread coal cinders to try to dry them. In later years when the high school football team played in Traction Park, the chance of plowing one's face in a batch of cinders was a greater hazard than the opposing fullback.

Although the performances varied somewhat from year to year, there were always exhibits, horse races, and ball games. The races featured sulky races, both trotters and pacers. Old Dad Greenleaf (in his seventies) was a perennial driver, white hair and beard streaming out behind as he went. Sulky races have always held a great appeal for me. I was fascinated by the tight control that a driver must have to get the ultimate speed out of a trotter without allowing him to break into a gallop. Even as a child I saw something really majestic about a big, powerful animal, nostrils blowing, and frothy sweat pouring from him, hurtling along with the little sulky and driver so close behind as to look as if they were riding on his rump.

A baseball game was held every day of the fair. Since fair week occurred after the national baseball series was over, big-league players were recruited to play with the local team, the Browns, and this provided two good teams and creditable baseball. The umpire

seemed always to be Tom Hubbell, the sheriff. He was a big man and was always dressed in a blue serge suit. He stood behind the pitcher to call strikes and balls, and also to umpire the bases. We had just one umpire, whereas today it takes two or three; but Mr. Hubbell was big and always wore his shiny gold badge. His decisions were not contested.

Most years a troop of cavalry from Fort Wingate, near Gallup, pitched camp on the grounds and gave daily exhibitions of drilling and horsemanship. They played a game with five horses and riders on a side, all trying to push a huge ball towards one goal or the other. The ball was as high as the horses and would be propelled towards a goal by a horse bumping into it with his chest.

The greatest event of the fair was a balloon ascension. The huge bag was inflated with lighter-than-air gas that was produced by pouring kerosene on a wood fire. We kids got free admission to the fair to help anchor the balloon and keep it from sailing off prematurely by holding on to ropes attached to it. As it filled, it rose majestically into the air, covered with colored streamers and spangles. A large basket was attached to the balloon; the balloonist would mount it, we would release the tethering ropes, and it would shoot into the air amid cheers, a tune from the band, and colored paper thrown out by the balloonist. After it got to what seemed a terrible height the balloonist would jump out to parachute down, maneuvering the parachute so as to land in front of the grandstand. The balloon, freed from the man's weight, would slowly turn bottom up, emitting gas and smoke and eventually crash to earth, to be retrieved for the next ascension.

One year there was a death-defying act in which a beautiful black horse climbed a ramp to the top of a tower some seventy feet high and, with a daredevil on his back, dove into a tank of water seventy feet below. One day $100 was offered to any local citizen who would ride the horse until he emerged from the tank. A

grocery clerk named Riley Edwards, who was conveniently quite bowlegged, made the ride and collected. He was the town's hero for weeks.

We had several ways of getting into the fair, not counting the remote possibility of buying a ticket. One was to assist with the balloon; another was to help clean the racehorse stables; sometimes we got a job selling pillows to relieve tender derrières from the wear of hard bleacher seats. When all other means failed, we would sneak in.

The board fence around the fairgrounds was too high for a boy to reach the top unaided, so we worked in pairs: one boy leaned over, furnishing a platform from which another could reach the top and swing up. He could then reach down and pull up another. This worked fine unless a guard happened to be there, prepared to grab someone when he jumped down. If caught, a boy would be marched to the county jail house, lectured, and finally released—necessitating his having to go through the fence-climbing routine all over again. After all, fair time was fun time for children, adults, performers, and even guards. No one took too seriously a custom which has come down from time immemorial—of youthful illegal infiltration into show places.

There were no carnival concessions at the fairgrounds; these were allowed to set up in the side streets entering Railroad Avenue from Second to Sixth streets. They were open at night when all vehicular traffic on these intersections stopped. The merry-go-round, ferris wheel, and all other such attractions would locate back of the curfew at Second Street and Railroad Avenue. All daytime activity was at the fairgrounds, but nighttime revelry centered downtown around the carnival concessions. This enabled us to participate in the night's activities without having to venture into the darkness and uncertainties of the fairgrounds. It was also a boon to the downtown merchants and saloons, as they stayed open until the carnival attractions closed down.

In the carnival tents, we saw our first motion picture, *The Great Train Robbery*, first marveled at the sword swallower, the 350-pound fat lady, the living skeleton, the snake charmer, the tattooed lady, and by dint of sneaking in, our first "hootchie-cootchie" dancer—this latter for adults only. Every night, Monday through Friday, was fair night, with curfew hours suspended, and with lights and excitement on every hand. Then, on Saturday night, Railroad Avenue was closed to traffic from First to Sixth streets; everyone was supposed to be in masquerade dress, bands played, and people danced in the street and threw confetti and paper streamers. When the hilarity was over at midnight, the street was a shambles and the people were disheveled, but as they walked home, arm in arm, some sober and some not so sober, they sang and were wonderfully happy. It was the end of another fun time, memorable and happy.

I was twelve or thirteen when I became acquainted with the Colombo Hall on North Second Street. It seemed to play a prominent part in my early Albuquerque. The hall part was in the second story of a building, over a full basement, and consisted of a large dance floor with a stage at one end and a small balcony at the other. One got to the hall by climbing an impressive number of cement steps. There seemed to be something of a mystery about what went on in the basement rooms, but the hall was the scene of many functions that we were permitted to attend. I can remember glee-club performances, minstrel shows, and plays, but my strongest remembrance is of an outstanding demonstration of wireless telegraphy.

There I learned that Guglielmo Marconi, an Italian working in his homeland, had discovered that a machine could be made to project an electrical impulse into the air, causing some sort of air wave that could be received by another machine at a distance, and effect all kinds of wonderful results. At any rate, that is the understanding I got of it all. Mr. Marconi and his friends foresaw great things for this wireless phenomenon if they could get the money to develop it, and they were trying to interest people to buy stock in a company by giving demonstrations. The Albuquerque demonstration was held in Colombo Hall and we kids were there.

Elaborate machines had been set up in the balcony, with another group on the stage, about seventy feet away. The audience sat on chairs placed on the dance floor. In the demonstration, a man pressed a button, or something, up in the balcony and, presto, an electric light turned on on the stage, or a telegraph key chattered, or a bell rang. A lecturer went to great pains to assure us there were no wires from the balcony to the stage—that the electrical impulses went through the air over our heads to activate the gadgets on the stage.

Everyone seemed greatly impressed and I presume much stock was sold. Years later wireless telegraphy, radio, radar, and television grew out of this small beginning. I have always felt I was privileged to be in on the ground floor of one of the world's greatest scientific developments.

Of continuing interest at Colombo Hall were the Saturday night dances. Why we became interested in watching dances, I do not know, unless it was that they were a gathering of performing people, which was free, inside out of the cold, and probably most important, offered refreshments. I can't remember our having been welcome as spectators at dances at the Commercial Club or the Alvarado, but we were welcome at the Colombo Hall. I'm certain the dancing there was typical of the dancing at the time; that is, it was considered an exercise in grace rather than the athletic contests it often resembles today.

Dancing seemed an affair of man and wife, or young man and sweetheart. Dances were scheduled by program, the male taking the responsibility of having both his and his partner's programs filled with satisfactory partners for each dance. In this way he had control of who danced with his partner and could prevent her having to dance with someone distasteful to her, or to him. Each program included a few schottisches and polkas, but most were

two-steps and waltzes. Waltzes were the most popular, and afforded the supreme opportunity to demonstrate control and grace. Lively competition developed each Saturday night, and over the entire winter season, to determine which couple was the best. It was a formal competition, judged by a panel of their peers, and was the cause of much good-natured rivalry. The competitive dancers were announced late in the evening, giving competing partners a chance to get together, and to obtain a glass of water to be placed on the man's head. This was to assure he danced smoothly, without bouncing and jerking, else the water would spill or the glass crash to the floor. Those who were not competing would retire to the sidelines to encourage their favorites. At the end of the dance, the judges announced the winners and there were congratulations, laughing, treating, and a generally hilarious time—and refreshments! During the winter there were eliminations pointing to the season's finale. This engendered as much exciting competition as did the annual bicycle races, the horse races, and the baseball series.

By the time I entered the University in 1912, the precision and grace of the waltz had lost its attraction and the one-step had taken over. Although we had to develop the dexterity to negotiate the rambling one-step without treading on our partner's toes, I can't remember anyone getting a prize for smoothness and grace, nor did we attempt to dance with a glass of water on our heads.

Also, there was no dance hall at the University so the school dances were usually held downtown in the Women's Club building, across the street from the synagogue. Because of lack of transportation, groups of boys and girls could be seen walking down the hill—the boys in blue serge suits and the girls in flowing evening gowns—all wearing old shoes and carrying their shiny dance ones. They would change shoes for the dance and change back to the hiking ones for the trip up the hill. This would seem an impossible hardship today, but in those days it was all part of the fun.

9

DURING MOST OF THE TIME we lived on North First Street, my sister and I lived alone. Later, my father came down from Algodones and we moved again to North Fourteenth Street in a one-and-a-half-story house, south across the street from the Harwood Home for Girls. Behind our house on Fourteenth Street, in a vast open space before the first houses of Old Town, was a brick-making enterprise.

Modern pressed brick are made by subjecting molds of moistened clay to terrific pressure before placing the resultant brick into previously constructed gas-fired kilns. Before this marvel of mechanization—even back to Biblical days—brick had been made in a much cruder way. Mud was slammed into a mold by hand, and the resultant brick dried in the sun before burning. These were called common, or "pug-mill," brick because the mud was mixed in a huge box called a "pug-mill."

The mud was churned in the pug-mill by mixing paddles, turned by a long boom that a team of mules pulled round and round. When it was well mixed, a portion was allowed to ooze through a

porthole near the bottom of the box. A "molder" grabbed the chunk, kneaded it much as dough is kneaded in making bread, and slammed it into the mold, one of three brick-sized cavities in a three-mold box. Bearers then carried the mold and dumped it, leaving three mud bricks to dry in the sun. I served for a time as a "bearer," for which I received ten cents an hour for a ten-hour day. I can strongly recommend this job for one in training as a football player.

When the brick were dry, they were placed in a huge stack (a kiln) in a manner that permitted the heat from fires in its base to circulate through the entire stack.

Albuquerque depended on these brick in 1899 and until pressed-brick plants were started. They are soft compared to the pressed brick and break more easily, but their porosity creates a pleasing quality, and with age permits them to acquire an attractive patina. Most old brick houses in Albuquerque are built of these brick and, when one is torn down, there is a demand for the brick at premium prices.

We saw Halley's comet while living on Fourteenth Street this time, in 1910. For days before the event, the papers carried lengthy articles about it, giving predictions as to the exact time it would occur, streaking across the northern sky, traveling from east to west. We wondered then, as I still do, how they could predict so accurately a phenomenon of the celestial bodies. Halley predicted the comet would appear again in 1986, and I hope to see it.

Two newspapers were published in Albuquerque, the *Journal* in the morning, and the *Evening Herald.* The *Journal* occupied a low building on the south side of Gold Avenue, midway between Third and Fourth streets. As the lot east to Third was vacant, the side of the building was exposed, and on it they had erected a huge bulletin board and thermometer. The *Journal* staff posted bulletins on the board, essentially performing the functions now furnished by radio and television: providing prompt news on baseball scores, the outcome of prize fights, election results, war reports, and lists of those killed in action. During the World Series, a crowd would gather to follow the game reported by these bulletins.

The *Journal* stands out vividly in my mind because I was a carrier for several years. We reported to the office at 5:00 A.M. to get forty to sixty papers and carried them in a neck-sack fore and aft. I rode a bicycle to deliver the *Journal.* Our pay was ten dollars a month, less deductions for "kicks" if a customer reported a failure to deliver his paper.

We moved again, into a brick house between Fourth and Fifth streets on Tijeras Avenue. The Springer Transfer stables, which occupied most of the block where the County Court House now stands, were across the street. I'm sure that our many moves were not made to give me new experiences, but that was their effect. Living across from Springer's enabled me to learn more about horses, and to know Bill Springer. He was a remarkable character, indeed: a frightening character to a boy at first, but wonderfully kind nevertheless. A large, red-faced man with a bull voice and an impressive vocabulary of swear words, he was the boss, no mistaking, omnipresent in body and voice. He ran a taut ship; everything had to be in place; the horses curried, brushed, fed, and harnessed on schedule, and just so. Everything had to click. He particularly loved his horses, and he had some magnificent specimens.

I later worked for Mr. Springer as the driver of a dray. For some reason he assigned to me, a green lad, a team which included a large, mean horse called Shoestrings. He gave me detailed instructions about Shoestrings. I was afraid of the horse, but even more afraid that I would not follow Mr. Springer's instructions. One thing he particularly cautioned me not to do was to lead Shoestrings from the wagon with one tug still fastened to the singletree. If I did, he warned me, Shoestrings would tear me apart. Well, as fate would have it, I did just that, and Shoestrings proceeded to do his part. He swung me around like a leaf, kicking and pawing. Through it all I could hear Mr. Springer's voice, telling me to — — — hold on, or — — — he would kill me. I wanted to turn loose, but was afraid to, so I hung on until someone loosened the tug and things settled down.

As one grows up in a community, a fondness for its institutions develops. For me, the Springer Transfer Company has a special importance. No doubt this was due in part to my early experiences with Mr. Springer and the fine men associated with him: Louis C. (Benny) Bennett, Herbert McNama, Roy Strome, and others. My admiration for this firm was enhanced when they acquired the site of the old wool scouring mill and had built on it their new office and warehouse building. Instead of arranging for an ordinary warehouse-type of building in this outlying location, they displayed the courage and good taste to build an architecturally beautiful structure.

It stands today, a monument to the character of this organization. The firm has prospered greatly, and I rejoice to see it.

While living on Fourteenth Street and on Tijeras Avenue, I attended high school, where I associated with boys and girls who remained lifelong friends. Among them were Jack Lapraik, George

Walker, Pelham McClellan, Harry Frank, Louis Hesselden, Bob Wigley, Viola Blueher (who married Kenneth Baldridge), Lola Neher, Evelyn Everitt (who became Mrs. Edmund Ross), Lydia Craxberger, Walter Berger, Leslie Briggs, Don Wilson, and Bark Kee.

Bark Kee was a Chinese whose father, Sam Ho Kee, ran a sundry store on South Second Street. I visited in their store often and I always enjoyed inhaling the ever-burning incense. Mr. Kee kept books in Chinese script, which struck me as a most incomprehensible conglomeration of characters. The Kees later returned to China, and I often wonder what has happened to my friend Bark in the turmoil that has developed there.

While on the subject of the Chinese in Albuquerque, I should mention one who ran a laundry on South Second Street next to the Scheer Furniture Store. He laundered and ironed anything from a pair of socks to a stiff-bosomed dress shirt. We would watch his cute trick of sprinkling a garment for ironing by blowing a mouthful of water in a misty spray over the area to be ironed. One time, when we had a school play in the Crystal Theater next to where the post office had been on South Second, we wished to create a stage setting to resemble an Albuquerque street scene. Someone conceived the novel idea of "borrowing" signs from store fronts in town to hang on the mock store fronts on the stage. The effect on the stage scene was original and pleased the audience, but midway in the first act of the show, there was a loud commotion at the theater entrance as the Chinese laundryman came storming down the aisle, gesticulating wildly and shouting unintelligibly, all to the effect that he wanted his sign. We stopped the show and gave him his sign, whereupon he left peaceably enough, but still muttering. I can't remember anything about the show, but I can remember hearing remarks to the effect that the best part of it was the performance put on by the Chinese laundryman.

The high school occupied part of the second floor of the Central School building. All sat in one assembly room, the freshmen in the first rows, the sophomores in the next few, and then the juniors and seniors in about two rows each. We sat at ordinary school desks, with the inkwell in the corner and a shelf for books underneath. In addition to this assembly room, there were two classrooms, the office of the superintendent of schools, and one for his secretary.

Other high-school classmates were Bill Grimmer, Dave Weiller,

Arthur Yanow, George and Anna Myers, and Norine Switzer. The two Tompkins girls were in school then. Pearl Tompkins later married Charlie Weber and Bunney became Mrs. Charles Lembke.

In my freshman year, a school yearbook was initiated, and we were asked to put proposed names for it in a suggestion box. I submitted the name of *La Reata* (The Lariat), and, as it was the only suggestion made, it became the name of the Albuquerque High School annual—my only claim to fame.

Fred Calkins was a junior when I was a sophomore, and he instigated the formation of a high-school football team. We furnished our own suits and gear (such as they were); the coaches were volunteers from town. We practiced after school on a nearby vacant lot, dressed in a large closet in the building and had no shower, doctor, or trainer. We played for fun. Frank Shufflebarger, Louis Hesselden, Bill Grimmer, Jack Lapraik, Bob Wigley, Otto Scheer, and Arthur Bachechi were some of the players on that team.

The courses taught in high school were strictly academic—no dancing, sewing, or commercial courses. Those who desired to train for the world of commerce usually transferred to the Albuquerque Business College, which occupied the second floor of the Korber Building and was run by Mr. Joe Goodell. One who chose to do so was Florence Gustafson, a dimunitive Swede, the joke editor of *La Reata*. She eventually became a key assistant to Mr. C. N. Cotton in his mercantile establishment in Gallup.

The abbreviation for the Albuquerque Business College was, of course, A.B.C., a designation very dear to the graduates of the school, but we high-school students quipped that the initials stood for what was taught over there. We did not, however, speak so disparagingly of the A.B.C. basketball team, as they were stellar performers and beat all comers. Walter Galles, brother of the immortal Herbert (Fat) Galles of University of New Mexico football fame, played on that team.

An unforgettable character connected with the high school, and one whom we all loved, was Colonel Ed Johnson, the janitor. He could always be found in the basement, where it was cool in summer and warm in winter, and where any of us were always welcome to sit and chat. He was a Civil War veteran of the Union Army, but his talent for storytelling was not dimmed by age. Although old and gray and trembly, he would address the student body once or twice a year, telling us Civil War stories. Colonel Johnson also had a supply of tin cups, plates, and spoons stored away in his sanctum; and when we could successfully raid an ice-cream party at night, we would carry the ill-gotten booty to the high-school basement, where we would find a supply of eating utensils, and Colonel Johnson's good-natured hospitality.

John Milne became principal of the high school after Mr. Joseph A. Miller resigned. I remember him as standing uncertainly on inadequate-looking legs, giving the impression that a stiff breeze would blow him over. In the opinions of the students, to these apparent physical incapacities, was added the inexcusable fact that he wore a derby hat. We were very uncertain about this character who had come to supervise our school until, during a football game in which we were playing Menaul School, and winning, we saw Mr. Milne beating his derby hat on the goal post and yelling louder than anybody. That did it. He was a made man from then on.

Mr. Milne was a made man in other ways, too. At that time, a man by the name of W. D. Sterling was the superintendent of Albuquerque schools. I can't remember what happened to Mr. Sterling, but suddenly he was gone; the School Board promptly chose Mr. Milne to succeed him. He established a record in public service by retaining the position for forty-five years. All this time he was a wonderful friend to boys and girls, and I'm certain he demolished many imaginary derby hats on the goal posts of their victories.

Among the teachers I remember in high school were Mr. Miller (he made algebra seem easy), Miss Nancy Hewitt (she tried to make Latin seem easy, but that was too much to expect), Miss Elsie McLain, Mrs. La Rue (she was a wonderful teacher), and Mr. Levi A. Papineau. These wonderful teachers have long since passed on, and surely the Celestial Supervisor has assigned them a prominent spot befitting their great and worthy service.

In 1908, shortly after the U.S. Forest Service was authorized, a regional office was located in Albuquerque to administer the national forests of New Mexico and Arizona. Nearly all graduates in forestry then were from eastern universities, particularly Yale, so the Albuquerque office was staffed with a group of bright, young, recent graduates of these colleges. The introduction of these handsome young eligibles, wearing the glamour of their eastern origins, into the society of a western town of ten thousand souls, created a titillating stir among its young ladies. Even we boys looked up to them with something akin to hero worship. I can remember many of them: Frank C. W. Pooler, R. P. A. Johnson, Messrs. Fred Miller and Vernon Slonaker, and A. O. Waha and his delightful younger brother, Howard Waha, who could sing sweetly, dance (so the girls said) "divinely," and play tennis superbly. I worked for Howard Waha years later on the construction of the Red River Hill road. Aldo Leopold, a pioneer ecologist, was also one of the foresters who came to Albuquerque.

The attractiveness of the young ladies of a western town was sure to spark romance. Before it was all over, Lolita Huning had married Mr. Pooler; Mary Simms had married A. O. Waha; Aldo Leopold had chosen Miss Estella Bergere as his bride; and our high-school classmate, pretty Fannie Pratt, had caught our volunteer football coach, R. P. A. Johnson. I have no doubt there were other nuptials resulting from East meeting West which I don't recall, but I do remember that the "big one," in the person of Howard Waha, got away (only to be landed later by a pretty girl named Henrietta, from Ravenna, Ohio).

A two-story red brick building on the corner of Railroad Avenue and Edith Street had the appearance of having been a school of some kind, but I remember it with affection as the Albuquerque Public Library. It had a great influence on my life. On the ground

floor were large unoccupied rooms. A long flight of stairs ascended to the second floor, where two large rooms housed the library. The north room held the bookstacks, and the south room was filled with tables and chairs to serve as the reading room. In winter, each room was heated with a large, potbellied, coal-burning stove. A spacious lawn surrounded the building, the whole encompassing a quarter of a city block.

The library afforded my sister and me a livelihood for several years. My sister, Marion, served as librarian, and I was what the city directory chose to call the "custodian of the grounds and buildings of the Albuquerque Public Library"—in other words, the janitor. In the morning, after I had completed the *Journal* route, I would stoke the fires and sweep out. Dusting the books was a most odious job in the days before vacuum cleaners. My pay was thirty dollars per month during winters, but in summers, when I also attended to the grounds, I received sixty dollars per month. It is said a good library is a great aid to education. The Albuquerque Public Library was certainly an aid to my education: without those jobs for my sister and me, I could not have gone to school.

10

THE ALBUQUERQUE JOURNAL once printed the query, "What would you do if you had a million dollars?" and a wag who signed himself T. B. Crab answered, "I'd buy a windshield for Albuquerque." This witticism carried with it a suggestion of the awful truth as well as humor. The wind does blow in Albuquerque, especially during March, April, and May—to the point of distraction for the sick and the elderly. It seemed to pep up us youngsters. When it blew so hard that schools had to close, we would go hunting, or undertake other outdoor activities to challenge the elements.

The effects of wind are no longer as distasteful as when the village had relatively few structures, facing dirty streets, and nestled in a valley surrounded by vast stretches of unprotected sandy soil. When the wind comes, blowing sand begets blowing sand. Each particle, as it is dislodged, serves to scour and dislodge other particles, until the air is full of wind-blown sand that tears at structures, penetrates cracks, windows, and doorways, and lodges in one's ears and eyes. A story that circulated in the early 1900s told of the health seeker who built a little frame house out on the

mesa, but made the mistake of leaving a knothole in the west wall. The sand-laden wind blew through the knothole until it wore out the entire house. There was, and still is, an offsetting effect of sandstorms that loyal citizens and the Chamber of Commerce were wont to dwell on. In a country where the annual rainfall rarely exceeds nine inches, most of it falling in downpours in July and September, the atmosphere is not purified by the washing effect of periodic showers. A sandstorm, according to their promotional contention, cleans the air even better than rainfall, without creating excessive humidity. The morning after a sandstorm, the atmosphere did seem benevolently clean, and one could breathe in great gulps of "dry-cleaned" air. Now that the little village is covered with acres of houses and a blessed blanket of lawns and trees—bordered by miles of paved streets—the wind, although it tries valiantly, is not so successful in dislodging that original particle of sand. Its force still buffets the trees and flags and ladies' dresses, but it does not carry the tons of sand that housewives had to contend with in the early 1900s. And besides, by putting it through a vacuum cleaner, they now make the wind that brings in the sand take it out again.

The view of the western horizon has changed little since I first came to Albuquerque; the five volcano cones across the river made the western sky a complement to the eastern horizon, where the Sandia Mountains "lifted their heads on high." They were a never-ending conversation piece, and furnished extraordinary beauty "piercing the sunset sky." They even furnished a descriptive note in the Alma Mater song of the University (since rapaciously abandoned for some nondescript substitute). The volcanos were, of course, extinct—but were they, really? One time, some pranksters lugged a quantity of old rubber tires through the twelve miles of sandy country leading to the volcanos, and set fires in two of the cones, causing a dense cloud of black smoke to rise in the western sky. This caused considerable consternation, and people began to wonder whether the volcanos were awakening from their centuries-old nap.

In later years, we had an Estonian housemaid, a recent arrival from a German concentration camp. One day she asked my wife about those hills on the western horizon. When told they were extinct volcanos, she said, "What a country I am now in! Has volcanos doesn't work."

The passage of time has brought about many changes in the world, but perhaps the most pronounced change that has occurred in any given decade was brought about by the development of the internal combustion engine. Among other things, it led to the replacement of horse-and-buggy transportation by automobiles and trucks—and to the construction of good highways. In retrospect, these changes seem to have occurred abruptly, but actually, it was a slow, uncertain, and groping development. Years of trials and failures occurred before the "horseless carriage," which Tom Insley tried to drive through the sand of Tijeras Avenue, developed into the seven-passenger wonder that he drove, as a trusty, while chauffeuring for the penitentiary warden, Tom Hughes.

The struggle to attain automotive excellence went on in faraway places, like Detroit, but we saw the results in Albuquerque as shiny new models slid off freight cars to be introduced to admiring prospects by optimistic dealers—Buicks, Dodges, Chevrolets, Pierce Arrows, Winstons, Cords, Hudsons, Studebakers, Locomobiles, the Brush and the Peerless—it is said in all over 150 models were made. Finally, the car that enabled almost everybody to put his horse to pasture, the Model T Ford, proliferated throughout the countryside like weeds.

In time, pitifully primitive cars that could travel no faster than we boys could run gave way to mechanical marvels capable of speeds up to forty miles an hour. This created a demand for roads. The venture into the untrodden field of improved road construction—making them ever straighter and smoother, with ever-more-negotiable grades and dust-free surfaces—followed closely the slow and groping improvement of automobiles, and this struggle went on all around us. It was slowed down further because the cost at first had to be paid for out of already overburdened property taxes—until New Mexico's political genius, Charles Springer, conceived the idea of the gasoline tax. This idea, quickly adopted throughout the country, made those who used the roads pay for them.

Typical of this state-wide, in fact nation-wide, struggle were the

tortuous stages of development of the road from Albuquerque to Santa Fe. It came about in what might be termed four "generations" of roads. The first generation was the horse-and-buggy trail that followed the valley to a point opposite the pueblo of Santo Domingo. From there it wandered across a sagebrush flat to a ford across the Galisteo Creek, at the foot of an escarpment known as La Bajada with a hill-hugging route, around hairpin turns, and up steep grades.

Automobiles demanded something more. The second generation effort included widening and smoothing this original trail, along with making some improvement of alignment and grades. This helped travel by Model T Fords, but larger cars still had to round the curves on La Bajada by first going forward, then backing, and then going forward again.

It was eventually decided the valley route presented so many disadvantages that it was abandoned in favor of the third generation development—a route through the hills northeast of Algodones. After climbing hills and crossing arroyos, this route finally surmounted the highest ridge through a picturesque and somewhat frightening cut, one that can still be seen on the horizon from the present road. This route ended at the same crossing of the Galisteo, and climbed the same route up La Bajada, which had gained much notoriety by this time.

A mid-generation improvement was the relocation of the ascent of La Bajada midway between the original one and that with which we are familiar today. After that, it was rumored that a Peerless car had made the run to Santa Fe in two hours, but it seemed impossible. Real hazards on this road were the arroyo crossings, and many tragedies occurred when flash rains swelled them to dangerous depths.

It was not until after the period with which this narrative deals that the fourth generation developed. An engineer set up his instrument on the plain east of Algodones, pointed it north and then south, and announced the dictum that the new and final (?) generation of the highway when completely surfaced would follow the line of these sights, ironing out hills, and bridging arroyos.

This tortuous development of a highway connecting the state's capital and its principal city was not unqiue. The difficulties of finally surmounting Raton Pass between New Mexico and Colorado would make an interesting story. Similarly, the original attempt at a roadway between Albuquerque and Socorro and Las Cruces labored through the hills east of the Rio Grande valley and over a section of the ancient Jornada del Muerto, presenting a harrowing experience to those attempting it in a car. To get to Gallup from Santa Rosa, one had to go by Las Vegas and Santa Fe to Albuquerque and Los Lunas, then west. These early routes were relocated and improved when people insisted on new roads for the better and faster automobiles being produced.

The changes brought about by automobiles, trucks, and good roads were vividly apparent in New Mexico. In the early days, by horse and buggy, Bernalillo was a long day's journey from Albuquerque; Santa Fe was two days; and Las Vegas, three days away. Each town that was the center of a considerable population was of necessity an independent commercial entity, with at least one general store that could furnish anything from a pin to a piano. Las Vegas was the trade center of a vast northern area, and hence the home of large wholesale merchandisers—Gross Kelly and Company and the Charles Ilfeld Company. Gallup, with the C. N. Cotton and Gallup Mercantile Company trade empires, filled the needs of the western part of the state. Large stores in towns south and east took care of the needs in those parts, independent of Albuquerque. After the development of fast highway transportation, it was inevitable that a central point for warehousing and wholesaling would emerge—one that was in a central location, on a main railroad, and accessible from all points in the state. Albuquerque had all these advantages, and it became the merchandising center for most of the state.

Fast automotive travel became possible—thirty minutes to Bernalillo, two hours to Santa Fe, three or four hours to Las Vegas or Gallup—and more and more people came to Albuquerque to do their serious shopping, while relegating to the stores in outlying towns the furnishing of day-to-day needs. Many of the big wholesalers moved their businesses to Albuquerque. This had an astonishing and, in some respects, an unfortunate effect. Albuquerque developed and grew prosperous, while many of the formerly prosperous towns shrank in population and came upon hard times. Some resentment and bitterness towards Albuquerque developed, persisting even until today. This seems the lot of many large and prosperous cities in all states. They suffer the bitterness of unpopularity along with the sweets of success.

All this economic development, as well as the political development within New Mexico, had little or no impact on us while we were young. As time went on, however, and our comprehension grew, we became vaguely aware that New Mexico was only a territory within the family of states—a sort of stepchild—and we finally came to understand the disadvantage to the cultural, economic, and political life of the commonwealth of this administrative abomination. Santa Fe was our territorial capital, but it had an aura considerably out of proportion to its authorities under a territorial system of government.

Fortunately, many able and patriotic citizens in Albuquerque and in the state continually brought pressure to bear on an uncooperative Congress to grant New Mexico its statehood. This final graduation from political youth to political maturity was attained in 1912.

During all this time I was growing up, and so was Albuquerque. When I was a boy of eight, Albuquerque was a village of about 5,000. When I matured to adulthood and entered the University in 1912, Albuquerque, including its effective population outside the restricted city limits, had matured to a city of 20,000 or more. As I grew out of short pants, Albuquerque's horsecars had given way to electric trolley cars; muddy streets became paved thoroughfares; concrete sidewalks were laid; and Railroad Avenue, which had connected New Town with its historic older sister, Old Town, had shed this realistic but colorless name and had taken on the geographically expressive one of Central Avenue. These changes marked Albuquerque's transition to long-pants days. It had emerged from a frontier town to a municipality; and in so doing it was changing from oxcarts to limousines, from high-heeled cowboy boots to patent leather shoes, and from frontier clothes to starched shirts and collars. The camaraderie and unadulterated fun of a small informal village had given way to the relative aloofness and dignity of a city.

A generation had passed, both in the lives of its people and in the progress of the town. In retrospect, I consider it a rare privilege to have grown up during this time with Albuquerque. There were those who came before, of course, and many wonderful folks have come after, but now that I have seen the village of 5,000 grow to a city of 350,000, I am even more appreciative of the citizens of that early period who built so well the foundation upon which such a splendid city could grow.

Thanks, Albuquerque, for what you have done for me. May prosperity and success continue in your history.

Index